Tales of Women Survivors

How We Became Free

Contributing Authors:

Katha Blackwell
Regina Butler-Streets

Natasha R. W. Eldridge
Lynn Fairweather, MSW
Shari L. Howerton

Catherine Mossman
Susan Peabody
Amanda Pearson
Rachel Russo, MS, MFT

Stephanie Snowe

Tales of Women Survivors

How We Became Free

Compiled by: Assuanta Howard
Edited by: Rachel Schade

ASTA
PUBLICATIONS

Compiler: Assuanta Howard
Editor: Rachel Schade
Cover Designer: Briana Salcedo

ISBN 13: 978-1-934947-88-3

This book is dedicated to you!

Contents

Introduction

I find that when you open the door toward openness and transparency,
a lot of people will follow you through.
-Kirsten Gillibrand

Senator Gillibrand's quote speaks about honesty, openness, and most of all, change. These are the traits *Tales of Women Survivors: How We Became Free* wants every reader to reflect upon. Many books are about sealing a story in history, but this compilation is about finding new beginnings and positive change. Each author is utterly transparent in her writing, offering real anecdotes and advice to women in challenging situations.

In the following chapters, there is a wide spectrum of personal struggles and routes to recovery. Each account encapsulates a different story of persistence, hope, and a path towards self-love. These chapters serve as a reminder that no one is truly alone, embracing a spirit of togetherness. Together, these stories inspire women to rediscover balance, happiness, and health in their lives.

A Note About the Authors

Asta Publications reached out to the contributing author after reading about their experiences in both published works and on personal websites. They come from all over the United States, and vary in expertise and backgrounds. But every author is passionate and excited about this compilation. The authors deserve the uptmost praise for their hard work throughout this publishing process, as well as for their eagerness to help women break free from unhealthy relationships.

Each author reopens a difficult chapter of her life in the following pages. In turn, we hope *Tales of Women Survivors: How We Became Free* will help other women put an end to difficult chapters of their own life stories.

Overcoming
Shari L. Howerton

I was raised in a performance-oriented church and home where the word "overcome" was synonymous with perfection. This understanding of the word overshadowed my outlook and choices for the first four decades of my life. But in my forties, God transformed my perspective and showed me that although I'm not perfect and never have been, I am already an overcomer.

I married at the age of sixteen, obviously a child. My groom, Dennis, appeared to be a full grown man, but was in reality a twenty-three-year-old child. Neither of us possessed a great deal of wisdom or maturity.

I certainly didn't recognize the warning signs that were clearly present. I eagerly joined my life to a narcissistic bully. As I attempted to adapt and be "the good wife" I was taught I should be, I became an enabler. Submission and compliance were the high feminine virtues I was encouraged to aspire to.

Our relationship became volatile the first week of marriage, with my husband's explosive verbal rage and physical assault. During our first fight as a married couple, Dennis quickly became aggressive. After chasing me into the bathroom, holding me against a wall and pulling his fist back, my new husband stopped short of hitting me. He assured me he was sorry for letting his anger get out of hand. He lost control, he said. But he didn't lose control. His goal was to demonstrate who had the power in the relationship—and who did not. His desired outcome was domination through fear and intimidation.

And he succeeded. In our twenty-seven year relationship, my injuries were not external. They were much deeper, penetrating my soul.

During those early years, it was not unusual for my husband to strike me with an open hand, push me against a wall, or knock me down to the ground. He would throw objects and slam doors so pictures fell off the walls.

During the earliest years of our marriage, I was a naïve, trusting teenager trying to get along with a troubled and complicated man who mistreated me almost daily. It's hard to remember specific details of how our fights started because we fought about everything and nothing.

He was emotionally demanding. I could never figure out how to satisfy him or anticipate what he needed from me. He had such a deep hole inside him that it could not be filled up. I realized many years later that he loathed himself and transferred that loathing to me. But at that young age, I was far from being able to comprehend the psychological dynamics I was living in.

I can't remember the number of times he abandoned me when he was angry. It was such a routine part of my life that I just learned to accept it. One night, though, stands out from all the rest. It was Christmas of 1978, our son Danny's first Christmas. Dennis got mad at me, blew up, and abruptly left us.

I took my baby to my parents' house and spent Christmas Eve there. Danny was the beloved first grandson and my parents did the best they could to make it a merry Christmas, but I remember feeling so alone. I was not only hurt and disappointed that my husband would miss our baby's first Christmas in order to display his petty anger; I was also extremely embarrassed.

Worse than any physical pain ever inflicted was the way my husband belittled me. It was demoralizing. When he pushed me and I fell to the floor, he laughed at me in flagrant contempt. I can still picture him standing over me with a smirk on his face because he was bigger than me and I was at his mercy.

Dennis mocked me out of his own insecurity. He was so emotionally needy that he did not want me to feel confident or self-reliant. If I ever did, he was afraid I might not need him. That's why any personal growth on my part was a threat. The insults, put-downs, and sarcasm were his ways of keeping me insecure. If he was in control of how I felt about myself, he could manipulate me to serve his agenda.

Early in the marriage, while I was in my teens and twenties, I didn't have the maturity or the wisdom to understand these dynamics. I was intimidated. I was afraid. I believed he had all the power and I had none. Filled with self-doubt, I often agreed that I was to blame for our problems.

He was an expert at verbal sparring, and I was no match for him. He frequently told me that my family didn't love or respect me, and he tried to alienate me from independent women friends. Through all of these tactics, he was able to keep me constantly off-balance, insecure, and fearful. He fostered a sense of self-worth within me when it suited him, and jerked the rug out from under me any time he felt like it.

He effectively invalidated anything I tried to say, making me feel that I had no voice. His constant, calculated mind games perpetuated my self-doubt. Despite all my attempts at honest communication, I never felt as if my voice was heard, except when he felt in danger of losing me. During these times, he would become attentive and open to self-examination just long enough to win me back. He would make desperate promises in those moments, promises he never kept but that always gave me hope of real change and held me emotionally captive. I was later surprised to learn that this phase, the "honeymoon phase," is a spoke in the wheel of abuse. This phase itself is abusive, because it raises one's hopes only to cruelly crush them again and again.

Dennis didn't have any respect for me. I didn't know how to set boundaries, let alone enforce them. I had never been taught how to stand up for myself. Compliance was the virtue everyone seemed to want from me. In my marriage to Dennis, I was required to do his bidding and serve as amusement, even when his humor was at my expense.

One afternoon in 1982, I was in the kitchen preparing a big dinner of turkey and dressing. I was washing a dish at the sink while celery and onions were sautéing on the stove. On a whim, Dennis walked up behind me and put his hands around my throat, cutting off my oxygen. I couldn't talk, but he didn't seem to get the message from my body language that I couldn't breathe. He squeezed my neck and laughed while I struggled to convey my distress with arm movements. It was a scary experience. Not being able to breathe, I remember my thoughts: *I'm going to die and he's laughing.* I lost consciousness and went completely limp in his hands. As he lay me down on the floor, my arm hit the handle of the sauté pan. Hot butter splattered and burned my legs. When I came to, I was convulsing from lack of oxygen, my legs were burning from the hot butter, and he was in my face yelling at me. I was disoriented, yet my first thought upon regaining consciousness was not to question him, but to question myself. *Why is he yelling at me? What did I do wrong?* I thought. This is how an abused person thinks: *I must have done something to cause what is happening to me.*

Once the disorientation passed, Dennis explained that he was just having a little fun. He stressed repeatedly that he had been joking around and thought it would be funny to pretend like he was choking me. But when I passed out, he got scared. Although this happened during a time when it was known among friends and family that we were having serious problems in our marriage, we were not fighting that day, and he had not intended to hurt me. He said his greatest fear was that if he had killed me, nobody would believe he'd only been playing. He was frantic as I was lying there on the floor. Even when he thought I might be dying, his thoughts were of himself. He wasn't afraid that he might have harmed or killed me! He was afraid he would be held responsible if I died!

The experience frightened me, but I laughed it off. It seemed like a blessing in disguise, because for the rest of the evening, he went overboard with kindness. Kindness was not something I enjoyed regularly and was comforting. He kept asking if I believed he had not meant to hurt me and apologized over and over. I assured him that I believed him and it was no big deal. This even became a funny story that we occasionally told to friends.

Looking back, knowing everything I know today, I don't find it amusing. What kind of man walks up behind an unsuspecting woman and squeezes her throat for a laugh? It was a sadistic way to have fun, but at the time I never thought about it that way. I was desensitized to the aggression because it had become such a familiar aspect of my young life. I believe to this day that he had not intended to harm me. He really did think it was funny. Even his humor revealed a dark side.

Dennis was like a Jekyll and Hyde. On a good day, in the right circumstances, he was a great guy and people liked him. He had a quick wit and cracked people up, including me. He could be charming and fun to be around. At times, he was genuinely warm, personable, and caring. But almost everyone who got to know him at a deeper level eventually saw his dark side. If he felt slighted, if he didn't get his way, or if his demands were not met, he lashed out in anger.

I am convinced that Dennis suffered from full-blown narcissistic personality disorder. A narcissist feels entitled to whatever he or she wants. Narcissists expect everyone to figure out what they want or need, even when they don't tell people specifically. When (not if), someone fails to meet their demands, wants, and perceived needs, that person becomes their enemy. With them, anything could be turned into an offense. Life with a narcissist is precarious even on the good days, because everything can change in an instant.

It was such a relief when I finally started to see, in black and white, that a true narcissist's behavior makes the victim feel crazy and overwhelmed with self-doubt. That was exactly what I had been living.

Dennis rejected anything construed as criticism or that even hinted at an inadequacy within him, and responded with hostility. Communication was not relational with him; it was one of the ways he mentally toyed with me. For him, everything was about winning. He even boasted to me occasionally that he was able to convince me I was wrong even when he knew I was right.

Narcissistic people are often perceived by others as having an over-inflated ego because of their outward displays of arrogance and entitlement. But narcissism is actually rooted in deep insecurity and is exercised through acts of conscious self-preservation. Dennis could not handle feeling inadequate or vulnerable, although he was extremely needy and fragile.

He had anger issues until the day he died. I believe a part of that was the simple fact that anger is an empowering emotion. It makes one feel strong and in control. With the exception of brief windows of humility and vulnerability, I watched him channel every negative emotion he experienced into anger.

He perceived needing people, including me, as a weakness. Therefore, he tried to deny needing anyone, including me. He once confessed that he was aware he pushed friends away before they could reject him, because he anticipated rejection and feared it. Being in control and having the upper hand was paramount to him as a way to protect himself from being hurt. His mother instilled this way of thinking in him at a young age and often cautioned him as a young adult not to let anyone hurt him, especially women.

Throughout the early years of our marriage, Dennis frequently reminded me of how lucky I was to be with him. I don't remember him ever saying that he was lucky to be with me. I never felt special to him. I never felt like he appreciated or valued me. I didn't feel loved. Instead, I felt taken for granted and abused. Perpetual emotional abuse results in extreme vulnerability and a fragile sense of self-worth.

In 1980, Dennis went on the Optifast diet after becoming morbidly obese in the first five years of our marriage. He lost over 150 pounds, and looked and felt better than he had in years. I became more insecure, believing that if he thought I was lucky to have him when he was at his worst, he would surely feel even more superior after he lost a lot of weight. I imagined he would think he could do better and dump me. After all, this man had routinely abandoned me many times before.

My self-esteem became lower than ever. I was in a dangerous place mentally and emotionally, but I didn't recognize it. I was twenty-two years old and had been in an abusive marriage for six years. Then one day, I ran into a childhood flame and got caught up in a flirtatious conversation. It was not about physical attraction; getting involved with a man other than my husband had never even been a passing thought. But I was emotionally aroused. I felt a rush of conflicting emotions in those moments. I knew the conversation itself was wrong, but it smothered my self-doubt by building me up. Nothing else happened that day, but later, the phone calls began. He just wanted to talk to me.

We weren't doing anything that wrong, I tried to convince myself.

He complimented me and made me feel desirable. I still remember how seductive his words felt and how weak my defenses were. It wasn't about being told I was pretty or sexy: I wanted to be loved, wanted, and needed by someone. I wanted to feel important, and he made me feel like I was a prize. Dennis not only neglected me and took me for granted, but he also never wanted to build me or my confidence up in these ways. He wanted me to view him as the prize and be afraid that he might leave me permanently one day.

This growing emotional attachment outside my marriage was wrong, and I felt guilty. But I didn't want the kind, validating words to end, and after all, I justified to myself, all we were doing was talking. I have never used drugs, but I've been told that some narcotics are so addicting you can try them once and be hooked. Kindness and affirmation were those drugs for me.

Although the act of adultery was not premeditated on my part, several of our romantic meetings were. I found myself consummating this relationship in a secluded area of a public park. I cried all the way home, begging God to forgive me. I promised Him I would never let it happen again.

From that day forward, I passionately tried to be the perfect wife. I feared that if Dennis ever found out, he would surely leave me. Maybe, I thought, if I could make him happy, he would know how remorseful I was and how much I wanted our marriage to survive.

However, the marriage did not survive. Then, after he divorced me and lived the life of a player for over a year, he pursued me with a vengeance and convinced me to remarry him.

Our second marriage began with a year-long honeymoon phase in which he seemed grateful for our reconciliation. But over time he reverted to the same abusive behavior he had renounced while trying to woo me back. I stayed eighteen years the second time and finally left when I lost every ounce of false hope I had been clinging to.

In those last years, he resorted to physical violence again. He went through a two-year-long psychotic depression that wreaked havoc on me emotionally and physically. I still stayed. He hit me when I dared to express that I was struggling to meet the demands of his illness, and then he threatened to take a gun to his head and blow his brains out. He said the words in rage and revenge, not in desperation or as a cry for help. I knew in that moment that he only wanted to hurt me, even after all I had sacrificed for him.

In 2002, my only son and daughter-in-law were married. Since narcissists view children leaving the nest as a loss rather than the natural progression of a family, Dennis directed more abuse at me. By this time, I was in counseling and attending college. I finally found the courage to leave and file for divorce. He was callous and arrogant when I told him I felt abused. "If you feel abused," he said, "you should run from me as fast as you can because you have it good."

It was good advice and I took it.

I'm now married to a man who loves, cherishes, respects, and values me beyond my wildest dreams. But I was so beaten down when I left my abusive spouse, I had no imagination of the life and blessings that would follow.

In March 2011, I watched Oprah Winfrey interview Meredith Baxter about her memoir, *Untied*. Even though many years had passed since I had left my ex-husband, her words resonated deeply within me, giving me goose bumps. Oprah brought up an example of physical abuse Baxter had shared in her book, then asked: ". . . the relationship was not as physically abusive as it was emotionally and verbally abusive, would you say?"

Meredith responded, "Right. And the truth is, you don't have to be abused physically too many times . . . a couple of times, and you know that's always on the back burner. That can always come. It's the continuing corrosive effect of being belittled, denigrated . . . I had no voice for so long."

In that moment I was flooded with memories and overwhelmed with emotion. I sat glued to the TV. As Baxter spoke, her voice broke, and I could see tears in her eyes. Here was someone most people would describe as a powerful, successful woman, and she knew precisely how powerless and helpless I had felt. I knew instinctively that she had experienced the same abuse, that her words were genuine. You never forget what it feels like to be treated that way. No matter how many years pass or how much you heal, you never forget.

There was more emotional and verbal abuse than physical abuse in my marriage, too. I never had injuries that required medical attention. I believe Dennis enjoyed putting a little fear in me from time to time. He was a bully. He wanted me to know who was in charge, just in case I ever doubted it, and I never lost sight of what he was capable of.

During the darkest days of my past, I remember asking God why He wouldn't do something to relieve my suffering. But I also remember focusing through my tears on Romans 8:28. I was aware that those who have suffered themselves have the most to offer another hurting person, and helping others was the desire of my heart.

I told the Lord on numerous occasions, "If the only good thing that comes from this is my ability to help someone else down the road because I truly understand this pain, that will be enough for me."

I didn't expect to do more than help a few friends through difficult circumstances. But God has redeemed my suffering in greater ways than I ever hoped for. As I was relating my story to a friend recently, I heard a still, small voice inside me whisper, "I gave you the desires of your heart."

About the Author
Shari L. Howerton

Shari Howerton is the author of two books focused on overcoming abusive relationships. In *Breaking the Chains*, she explores her life in a cultish church as well as the process of breaking away and overcoming years of spiritual abuse. In *Through My Eyes*, Shari relates the details of her twenty-seven years as a battered woman and her path to emotional health. In both books, she confronts the wounds of abuse and shares her deeply personal story of self-discovery, empowerment, and healing. Today Shari is happily married and lives in Daniels, West Virginia. She is increasingly a voice in her community for awareness. Recently she participated in two television interviews about the harmful message in *Fifty Shades of Grey*. (You can view it in this archive. Her interview is "Domestic Violence Survivor Speaks out about..." at http://www.wvnstv.com/video.) She is a passionate advocate for victims of domestic violence and volunteers her time, as well as donating the majority of her books' proceeds, to the

Women's Resource Center in her community.

For more about Shari and her writings, visit her website and blog at: www.sharihowerton.com and www.sharihowerton.blogspot.com.

The Hungry Heart
Susan Peabody

Change is important, and the process of change begins with honesty. Honesty is the willingness to admit out loud that you have a problem or weakness.

Honesty takes on an even deeper meaning when you tell your story. This is never easy, but as you listen to yourself describe your experience with weakness, you will gain a new awareness of how you got off track. This helps you understand what needs to be changed in order for your transformation to unfold.

Telling your story not only helps you, but also helps others. As people listen to you, they often hear their own stories and find out they are not alone. This dissipates their shame and jump-starts their transformation processes.

Today I am a professional writer and counselor. My book *Addiction to Love: Overcoming Obsession and Dependency in Relationships* has been on the market since 1989. My most recent book just came out; it is entitled *The Art of Changing: Your Path to a Better Life*. However, my life hasn't always been this great. As they say in the recovery community, I am a survivor, and I have been in recovery since 1982.

My drug of choice was romantic love. It kind of crept up on me. In the beginning, I was just an innocent looking for love. Then things got out of hand.

It all began when I was about ten years old and started falling in love. My first crush was a boy named Alan. Oh, how I loved him. I just knew he was going to make all my dreams come true, but Alan was embarrassed and angry that

I liked him so much. He told me not to write his name on my schoolbooks and threw rocks at me when I walked by his house. I can still feel the sting of those missiles. Humiliated, I cried, but nothing discouraged me.

Every day I watched Alan play baseball at the park. At school, during recess, I would sneak into the cloakroom and put on Alan's jacket. I wanted to touch something that was his—I wanted to smell his presence. I also wrote in my diary about my love for Alan. Day after day, I described the bittersweet pain of unrequited love, hoping that someday Alan would love me too.

There were other infatuations over the years. The pattern was always the same. I fell in love and believed that only this particular boy could make me happy. And I always felt so powerless—as if I couldn't help myself. Eventually, I would get emotionally and physically sick from yearning to be with someone I could not have. Then, when the pain became unbearable, the obsession faded and I found someone more promising to adore from a distance.

High school was not a happy time for me. I prayed that someone would ask me out on a date. One time I did get a call from a boy who asked me out, and I agreed to go. I was so excited and nervous that I stayed up all night making a new dress. The next day at school, some boys snickered at me as I walked by. That night a friend called to tell me that the phone call I had gotten the night before was just a joke. I was so embarrassed that I wanted to die.

When I was nineteen years old, I became desperate to have a relationship. I wanted to have a boyfriend and was willing to do anything to get one. However, I did not feel lovable enough to attract someone I really liked, and I was too impatient to wait for someone compatible to come along. Instead, I got involved with the first person who showed any interest in me.

While walking down a San Francisco street with some friends, I met Ray. I smiled at him, and he turned to talk to me. I left my friends to spend time with Ray. We ended up at his apartment, and I never left. Within a few months I was pregnant.

Ray was a pimp, who turned me into a prostitute. I had a high tolerance for suffering, because in my mind, this was the price I had to pay to have a man in my life. Because of my low self-esteem, I was willing to do anything to hold on to him, and I did not believe I could ever do better. Ray took advantage of this. He only came home when he felt like it. He didn't give me any affection. Ray and I didn't even talk very much, unless he was telling me what to do.

He took all of my money, except what went toward paying the bills. Sometimes I would try to hide money for a rainy day. Then Ray would get into some kind of trouble with gambling or drugs and beg me to give him some money. He said the men he owed money would kill him if he did not pay up. I can still see him standing there, tears running down his face, asking me to save his life. Of course, I always gave in. I felt responsible for him.

I also accepted a lot of dishonesty from Ray. I had no idea what it felt like to trust him. Usually he lied to me about other women, saying he was not having affairs. Deep down I knew what was going on, but I was afraid if I said something to Ray, he might leave me.

Of course, I wanted more than I was getting out of the relationship. I was too afraid to demand it. So I just cried when my birthday went unnoticed. When Ray didn't come home at night, I spent hours lying in the bed, curled up like a child, waiting for his car to pull up.

Despite my dependency, I tried several times to end my ties with Ray. After six months, I decided I wanted to leave him. When I told him, he got very sad. He said, "I guess you've gotten what you want and now you're ready to move on and leave me behind." I felt guilty when Ray said this, and I stayed with him to keep from hurting his feelings. I projected my fear of being abandoned onto him and assumed that he could not survive if I left him.

Later in the relationship, I thought about leaving Ray again, but I felt guilty about withdrawing my financial support. I knew Ray had become dependent on me. I was also afraid to leave the relationship because I knew it meant facing my fear of loneliness and giving up my identity as a caretaker. Most of all, I didn't want to face the emotional pain of breaking up. So I kept putting it off, hoping my misery would end someday.

A third time, I asked Ray to leave, but when he started packing his bags I panicked. The next thing I knew, I was begging Ray to stay—like a child begging her mother not to leave her alone in the dark. During this scene, my fear of abandonment overwhelmed me, and I was ready to do anything to avoid feeling the panic that gripped my heart.

Eventually, I became pregnant with our second child and Ray and I got married, because I did not want to be an unwed mother twice. During my pregnancy, Ray spent some time in jail. It was during this time that I fell in love with our neighbor and had an affair.

When Ray returned, I asked him for a divorce. Unfortunately, Ray was not ready to lose me. When I told him I was going to leave, he held a knife to my throat and threatened to kill me. Then he beat me up and held me prisoner in the house. He kept saying to me, "I know you still love me, just admit it." After three days of this, I agreed to stay with Ray and he immediately calmed down. I told him I had to get some food from the store. Ray agreed to let me go, and I quickly hurried out the door.

Once I was safe, I went to a phone booth and called the police. They told Ray to leave the house and he did.

The first man I got involved with after Ray was not much better, and that relationship failed too. From this point on, I became involved in a series of short-term relationships similar to the one I had with Ray. All of these relationships failed because I was too emotionally unstable to select an appropriate partner; and even if I did, I couldn't sustain a relationship because of my neediness, low self-esteem, and fear of abandonment. As the years passed, my hungry heart went unsatisfied, and this made me even more desperate to find love.

During these years of endless searching for love, I neglected my children. Kaitland and Randy were always important to me…in between relationships. I cooked their meals, washed their clothes, walked them to school, volunteered as a PTA mother, went to their sports events, and tucked them in at night. But when I had a boyfriend, things changed. I am ashamed to admit this, but I actually brought men I barely knew into the house to stay for long periods, and while these men were there, they became more important than my children.

Eventually, these toxic relationships and my guilt about neglecting my children took their toll and my health began to deteriorate. I developed a spastic colon and high blood pressure. I was chronically depressed and almost died in two car accidents. One occurred because I couldn't see the road when I was crying, and the other accident happened when I was fantasizing instead of looking where I was going. Finally, after another failed relationship, I was in so much pain I swallowed a bottle of aspirin while at a friend's house. I survived, but was in a coma for three days on my friend's couch before recovering. After this, I tried only one other time to end my life, and that attempt ended unsuccessfully too.

In 1982, my father died after having a stroke. The day

before he passed, I asked my boyfriend if I could use the car to visit my father in the hospital. My boyfriend said no, so I didn't go. When I cried about this in front of him, he promptly punched me in the eye. I guess he thought I was trying to make him feel guilty.

I sat at my father's funeral with a black eye and wondered what had become of my life.

After my father's funeral, I went to work, because I wanted to be a "brave little soldier." Across from me sat a co-worker named Barry. Barry had only recently been assigned to the desk near me after the office manager, for no logical reason, decided to move everybody around to new locations.

Around 4:00 in the afternoon I was typing away when I looked up to see Barry staring at me. I was curious about this and decided that it meant he cared about my situation—perhaps he felt sorry for me. This was good news for someone who felt invisible and unloved. I would take any kind of attention I could get.

I started stopping by Barry's office more often after this. It did not take long for me to fall in love. Eventually I asked Barry if he wanted to go out on a date. He very nicely said he was dating someone else. I was devastated, but undeterred. I decided at that moment that I would seduce him. Thus, in the blink of an eye, my final toxic attempt to find love began.

My master plan to seduce Barry was to lose weight and become so attractive that he could not resist me. I assumed men were basically weak when it came to sex. Over the next few months, I took off a lot of weight and spent all of my money on sexier clothes. Unfortunately, my plan didn't work. Barry was my friend and that was all.

To his credit, Barry never gave into my obsession to be with him. Instead, he only tried to help me with my depression. He never once mentioned my heavy drinking, which had become alcoholic by this time, or my dieting, which had gotten out of control.

One day, I was sitting in Barry's office and suddenly started crying. I turned to Barry and said, "Barry, can you die of loneliness?" I really thought he was going to tell me to stop feeling sorry for myself, but instead he looked at me with compassion and said to me, "Yes, you can die of loneliness. I know this firsthand."

I looked at him in astonishment, because after months of pouring out my heart to him he had never once told me anything personal about himself. Finally, after a long pause, he said, "Susan, I think you need to go somewhere where people understand you." That was it. No warnings about my alcoholic drinking or obsessive dieting—just a simple "get help."

I didn't visit Barry for a few days after this. When I did see him he asked me if I had gotten any help. I looked at him and blurted out, "No, I am afraid they might cure me." I was surprised at what I had said. Barry just laughed. It was only years later that I realized I had become addicted to the pain—the depression, the self-pity, and the misery. It was the only thread I had left, and I was afraid to let it go. The idea of happiness made me nervous.

Eventually, I did get help at a support group. At first, I didn't think my behavior was out of control, but as the facilitator explained how the program worked, something she said caught my attention. "You will have to learn how to ask for help," she announced.

"Not me," I said to myself with the assurance of a lonely, stubborn survivor. "I can take care of myself."

I had been attending the support group for about a year when Robin Norwood released her book, *Women Who Love Too Much*. Needless to say, I recognized many of my own obsessive behavior patterns. Enthusiastic, I looked around for a "Women Who Love Too Much" support group.

Unfortunately, there were none in my area. Undaunted, I started my own meeting for women who wanted to deal with the issues introduced by Robin Norwood. This seemed like a great way to promote my own recovery and at the same time offer other women the opportunity to turn their lives around.

A year after I began the group, when I was about a mile down the road to recovery according to Norwood's chart, I became interested in teaching others about the "disease" of loving too much. Armed with a teaching credential, a desire to be instrumental in helping others, and the support of my friends, I approached the principal of a local adult school. He was very enthusiastic about the general subject matter of the course I wanted to teach, but he encouraged me not to limit myself to just the issues presented in Norwood's book. He also wanted me to allow men in my class. When I agreed, he suggested I call my course "Addiction to Love."

Excited about the challenge of teaching, I set aside Norwood's book for a while and began reading other literature about obsessive behavior in relationships. This, of course, was a great learning experience for me. I was amazed to find out how much had been written about love, obsession, and dependency. Even Kierkergaard, as far back as the 1840s, wrote about the "habitual" nature of romantic love.

Once I had acquired a lot of professional information about love and addiction to supplement the information from my own personal experiences and the experiences of the women in my support group, I began to prepare an outline for my course. My goal was to condense and clarify many of the ideas introduced by others and then to interject some of my own concepts. By my own concepts, I mean an analysis of my own experiences. For example, in addressing the question of why some people become obsessive in relationships and others don't, most authors get around to discussing the debilitating effects of childhood deprivation within the dysfunctional home. Yet, none of them mention the devastating effects of peer rejection and how it relates to the creation of a lonely, needy love addict. Since this was a big issue in my life, I felt it was important to explore it a little further.

Also, none of the authors discussed the relationship between fantasizing and love addiction. To me, this is like talking about baking bread and forgetting to mention the yeast. Having been addicted to fantasizing as well as romantic love, I knew the connection between the two needed to be considered.

When I finally had a model, I taught my first class. It was an exhilarating experience, and my students' responses made it clear that I had valuable information about a serious problem. This is what prompted me to put my course outline into manuscript form and make it available to people who could not take the class.

Since *Addiction to Love* first became available, I have gotten a positive response from readers. They seem to appreciate the simplified concepts about obsession in relationships and the suggestions for change. Of course, I am very appreciative of this response and happy to be contributing in this way. Most of all, I am glad to be recovering from this disorder myself.

Today, I am still involved in helping other love addicts. In 2012, I celebrated thirty years of recovery and announced the publication of my latest book, *The Art of Changing: Your Path to a Better Life*. I am happier than I have ever been and enjoy helping others find their own recoveries. If you want to know more about me and my career, go to my website www.brightertomorrow.net.

While I might be embarrassed about some of the things I did in the name of love, I am proud of how far I have come in the last thirty years. If you also suffer from love addiction, I hope my story inspires you to change and reach out for a brighter tomorrow.

Since I wrote my story twenty years ago, I continue to recover from codependency and love addiction. Every day is a miracle. My greatest happiness comes from my work as a healer. The best decision I ever made was to become a teacher, because it has restored to me my lost, authentic self.

Currently, I am teaching at a treatment center and writing. I also travel the world, working with clients as a counselor. I recently got back from Switzerland, possibly the most beautiful country on the planet.

The hardest part of my life is choosing between being a paid professional and getting in line with my fellow love addicts. But I balance the two as best I can.

Let me close by saying that the best thing that has happened to me in the last thirty years of recovery was discovering spirituality. It grew out of my pain and suffering, and now it sustains me as I live life on life's terms. Over the years, I have lost my parents, my sister, my partner, my infant granddaughter and my beloved daughter. Without my faith in a benevolent force in the universe, I would have surrendered to the pain rather than looked to God for a brighter tomorrow.

Namaste.

About the Author
Susan Peabody

Susan Peabody is an author, educator, and counselor. Her books include *Addiction to Love* (2005), *The Art of Changing* (2005), *Where Love Abides* (2014), and *Recovery Workbook for Love Addicts and Love Avoidants* (2014).

For more about Susan and her writings visit her website: http://www.brightertomorrow.net/.

Growing From Grief:
How I Learned About Life From Experiencing Loss
Natasha R.W. Eldridge

When I was a little girl, I could not wait to be an adult. I had my life all planned out. I knew what I wanted and I was going to go after it. I looked forward to turning twenty-one, getting my own apartment and making my own way.

When I was a teenager, I worked extremely hard to make my dreams of becoming a happy and successful young adult a reality. I worked an average of thirty-five to forty hours per week throughout my junior and senior years of high school. When in college, as my dreams became more tangible, I made a conscious decision to acquire my own apartment in a desirable place, work full-time, and earn a Bachelor's degree in less than three years. I completed college a month before my twenty-first birthday, and I was elated to have accomplished such an ambitious plan. However, I had not accomplished success without my fair share of pain. It took a great deal of blood, sweat and tears to get past obstacles threatening my chance at success. Mid-way through college, I received a phone call that would forever change the course of my life. My father called me on Christmas evening, hours after I'd left my parents' home following a visit for the day. When the phone rang, I believed that it was my father calling to remind me that I didn't take any leftovers for the next day. I nonchalantly answered the phone only to hear my father's voice sound almost like a whisper. He asked me if I was sitting down. I was sitting, but I was puzzled by the question.

I answered, "Yes?"

He whispered, "Your Aunt Sandy was in a car accident this evening. She's in the hospital." He paused and I immediately burst into tears. Thoughts began swirling in my head. Guilt took over and I began to feel bad about not going to North Carolina for the first time in my life to celebrate Christmas. It would take us at least nine hours to get to the hospital. Before I could fully escape into my thoughts, my father continued," Uncle Malachi, Christal, and TJ were in the car too. They are all gone."

I don't recall any rational thoughts after that moment. I dropped the phone and screamed and cried in agony for hours. My world came to a screeching halt and there was absolutely nothing that I could do to "fix it."

Once my family and I finally reached North Carolina, the nightmare became more real. Although physically and emotionally broken, my Aunt Sandy was in relatively good spirits when I arrived. She clutched tightly to her faith to get through the funeral services for her children and husband. Her faith also guided her through her own recovery.

Admittedly, it was not that easy for me. I could not understand why this could happen to such a good family, on Christmas day of all days. They were singing Christmas carols when they were struck by the other car. In my mind, they could not have been more innocent or vulnerable.

I looked to my aunt's strength in an attempt to navigate through my own feelings of despair and anger. It wasn't easy. It took years for me to be alone with my own thoughts. I often heard the sound of the medical helicopter that transported Aunt Sandy from the hospital to the funeral of her children. I was often reminded of the small caskets that held my cousins' lifeless bodies.

I was nineteen years old, and until then the world was black and white. Good things happened to good people. Bad people were punished or reformed. The teenagers who carelessly ran the stoplight and murdered my uncle and cousins had no idea of the limitless potential framed in little bodies that they took away from this universe. I thought time would allow me to weather the storm. I believed things could not possibly get any worse. I couldn't have been more wrong.

I managed to hold my emotions together over the next year and a half. Aunt Sandy and I spoke weekly. I almost lost her once and it quickly taught me that life is short. I made sure that she knew I was there for her although I later came to realize that I gained so much more from our weekly conversations than any comfort or consolation I could possibly offer to her. We returned to North Carolina the Christmas following the incident. It was an emotional time for my family. Christmas was not the same. It was a joyous holiday overshadowed by the first anniversary of their deaths. Somehow we made it through the ashes.

May of the following year, Aunt Sandy made her first long trip to travel nine hours to my college graduation. She was proud that her niece was a college graduate in less than three years. I was proud that my aunt, my inspiration, pushed past her own pain to be there to support me. I could not have been happier. I quickly settled into my dream job, moved into my new condo and continued to speak to Aunt Sandy weekly after graduation.

Our second Christmas back to North Carolina was a little easier than the first. We somehow found an unspoken balance between sadness and celebration. We held each other tightly and laughed at old memories. Christmas evening, Aunt Sandy and I went to visit her family's gravesite. I choked back tears as I heard her speaking to her children and husband. She explained to them that she was trying to make it without them in this world. She explained to the children that no one could ever replace their daddy and that she waits for the day until they all meet again. We rode back to the family house in silence. We were beginning to put the pieces back together.

A week into the New Year, my father called me at work. He asked me to go home and call him when I got there. I knew by the familiar tone of his voice that I shouldn't ask any questions. I did as I was told. The fifteen-minute drive from Newark to Montclair, New Jersey took an eternity. I convinced myself that something had happened to my grandmother and attempted to prepare my emotions for the hit. My heart grew heavy as I dialed my dad's number. It almost felt like waiting to be hit by a train. You can never fully prepare yourself for the impact once you hear the train coming at you. My father asked that I sit down. I obliged. He told me that Aunt Sandy had been killed early that morning in a murder-suicide. She had been shot and stabbed multiple times in her own car. She was left to die in the middle of a field. The proverbial train was moving in slow motion. I don't remember much after that conversation either. I called a few close friends for comfort, but the pain reached unbelievably deep. I do remember feeling lost and dizzy, as if I were standing in the center of a tornado. In a flash, again, the world I had just put back together became unraveled.

I eventually underwent the five stages of mourning, but the process took its toll on me physically, emotionally and mentally. Eighteen years later, there are still things about that incident that I have never come to understand. However, I strongly believe that experiencing those tragic events as a young adult shaped me into becoming a stronger and more independent woman. Aunt Sandy was a free spirit who enjoyed her short life. She did not have an easy life, even before the death of her family, yet she always held her head high and smiled her way through her life's challenges.

For a very long time I believed with every ounce of my

soul that I could never gain the strength to overcome such an ordeal. I now pull from this experience when I find myself in a situation that seems insurmountable. My Aunt Sandy literally lost her entire family in a matter of seconds, yet she managed to smile and laugh while I visited her in the hospital days after. She held onto her faith when she had nothing else. *How can I dare act as if my world is ending when nothing in my life has been as horrible as what she was experiencing at that moment?* Although nearly two decades have passed, my feelings and memories about that time in my life are vivid and in some strange way feel tangible. It is almost as if I can reach into a proverbial handbag and pull out a dose of strength and positivity when I think about how I came out of sadness and anger to become a positive force in the lives of others.

While I was attempting to overcome the grief associated with the loss of my cousins and uncle, I decided to major in psychology while in college. I have always had a love for understanding people, working with children and helping guide parents to be better equipped to understand how their children learn and develop. I believe somewhere in our early twenties we all are hit with the desire to get to know ourselves on a different level. We cringe and when we look back at the decisions we made with our teenage minds, we vow that our twenties are going to be better. The tragedies forced me to dig deep within myself, to understand who I was and who I wanted to be. That was not an easy journey. I found myself clinging to every philosophical and psychological theory that I studied. I had to turn this tragedy into triumph. I had been forced to realize there were many things that were beyond our control. For goodness sake, my aunt was singing Christmas carols with her family when their vehicle was struck. Nothing could have been less predictable. I decided to turn my strengths and interests into something that would make a difference in the lives of others.

I started by exploring and deciding how I wanted to be remembered if I passed away prematurely. I wanted to create a legacy. If I were to suddenly leave this earth, I wanted to make sure that I lived my life in a way that it would matter that I existed at one time. I began by starting my career as a dropout prevention counselor for a nonprofit organization, volunteering my time and donating money directly to "at-risk" youth.

For me, working with children enables me to be able to see life from varying perspectives. Each perspective gives me insight into my own existence. I began to ask questions in order to challenge myself. How am I the same? How am I different? What successes, situations or obstacles had they and their families faced in their own lives that shaped their existence? What choices must I make in order to accomplish my goals? What decisions might hinder me from being successful? If I do this, how will it affect that? Looking at my life from a diverse perspective enabled me to forever be more introspective. At the time I thought I was simply keeping myself busy to keep myself from being down about missing my deceased family. I was so wrong. I was creating a new and better me. A more thoughtful, decisive and focused young adult was emerging. Had I not experienced such a great loss at that critical time in my life, I am confident that I would have had a more carefree attitude in my early twenties. My behavior would have likely been more reckless and I would have had to live with the consequences of those poor decisions. Although I despised the young men that stole the lives of my family, had it not been for their careless actions, I believe that I would have fallen victim to the invincible syndrome of which many twenty-somethings suffer. I knew better. I all too well understood that life was not forever. I looked at life as if time was always about to run out of the hourglass. I lived my life accordingly.

Now, no longer a young adult, I can look through a rear view mirror back at my twenties and I know that all of my major life decisions have been in part attributed to my conscious perspective on life. I am married with two phenomenal daughters, ages eight and ten.

I am a successful entrepreneur and still enjoy mentoring "at-risk" youth and young adults. It amazes me how much my life changed ten years ago. Although I had long come to accept the deaths of my loved ones, I had not really been able to truly empathize with my aunt's pain of losing her children until I had my own. Honestly, even the thought of losing them temporarily scares me. Every parent has that moment in a department store when their busy toddler decides to "hide" beneath the clothes on the rack. I recall my own experience when I was shopping when my daughters were six weeks and two years old. I had a cart full of items. My newborn was sitting in her car seat securely strapped into the cart and as fast as a blink, my toddler disappeared. She decided of all times, that moment was a good time to play hide and seek. I couldn't unstrap the baby fast enough. I "lost" her. She was no longer in my eye's view. I became instantly paralyzed. I had to get to her before she ran into danger or danger found her. I found myself playing a bunch of horrifying scenarios in my head as I tried to gain my composure and think of a game plan to find my baby.

My flow of irrational thoughts was suddenly interrupted. Thankfully, she couldn't contain her laughter, emerged from the pile of clothes and ran back to me seconds later. She was so happy that she finally was able to hide from me and I was unable to find her. All I could do was hug her. Those thirty seconds without her felt like an eternity. I tried to shake the feeling and I wanted to laugh and smile with her because she felt good about being a good hider. She was proud of herself.

She will not know how much she scared me until she one day has her own child.

I remember thinking on the way home from the department store that I was blessed to be able to be bringing both of my daughters home with me because I know that there are parents who are not that fortunate. I remember thinking what it must have been like for Aunt Sandy to have to come back to her family's house and look at her children's empty beds, favorite toys, book bags and clothes. Until I experienced what I viewed as the possibility of losing my daughter I had been caught up in the euphoria of motherhood. My new normal had me engulfed in nighttime feedings, dirty Pampers, hugs and cuddles, games of peek-a-boo and high pitched praises for the milestone achievements of my little ones. I became temporarily complacent and started to take the joys of life for granted. Both of my daughters have names that are derivative of my aunt's. I've shown them pictures and have spoken of her since they were babies. The department store incident readjusted my sense of perspective and reminded me that I needed to live in the moment as often as I could. It prompted me to remember that I wanted to be my best self at all times for few of us are wise enough to know when our last moment will be. *If, goodness forbid, I had forever lost my baby in that store would I be at peace with our last few interactions together?* The answer to that question would've been yes because we were talking and laughing as we were shopping. I saw how my aunt clung to the good memories and great times when I listened to her reminisce about how everyone loved her husband's chicken salad recipe or how the children loved their gifts on that last holiday. She had no regrets about their time together. She knew they loved her and they knew she loved them. With all other things considered, I think she felt good that their final cherished moments together were great.

As I work hard to create the legacy I desire and make the

people I love proud, I am fortunate that I was chosen to be the niece of such a great woman who, even after her passing, continues to bequeath valuable life lessons upon me. I could have easily become bitter and broken. The easy route would have been to always look at the glass as half empty and engage in self-destructive behavior because I was mad at the world for stealing so much from my family and me. Instead, I find joy in taking in the little things. Amidst the chaos of my life as a business mommy, I still find it important to take a day off from running my businesses to steal a day at the beach with my husband and our daughters on random Wednesdays in the summer. I enjoy being the silly class mom that bakes cupcakes and attends class trips so that I can gift memories of my presence during the school day with my girls.

I find peace in being comfortable in my own skin. I sleep well because I treat people as I desire to be treated. I work hard to listen without judgment. I enjoy the benefits of the rewards I have earned because I appreciate that without taking risks there will not be any rewards. I have failed miserably at times but I do not relish in regret, rather I take a very brief step back and search for a lesson learned. I look for a reason why I have been chosen to partake in the experience and how I will take control of the situation to make me a better me. I have always been genuinely happy for the success of others and find joy in watching or helping them to achieve their goals. I have a unique perspective on life and that has helped me to help others. It has also helped me to connect with people from all walks of life. I have learned so much from their experiences and I believe it is because I want to find not only the good in others but also I am genuinely interested in their life stories.

If someone looked at me when I was twenty-one and did not get to know my story, then they would not have seen my struggle to move beyond my pain. They would have seen a well put together young professional who owned a condo in a great neighborhood. They would have looked at a young lady who seemed wise beyond her years and never known that I was physically falling apart at the seams because I believed that life was too unpredictable and too painful to bear. However, with time the impossible does become possible.

Deep, open wounds do heal but one has to be open to the journey. Life is about how we overcome our fears to peel back the layers of our souls. It is about how we steal moments where we laugh so hard that our souls shake. Overcoming obstacles that seem insurmountable and being able to really reflect and learn from our rights and wrongs make us stronger and wiser. Suffering loss and finding a way to show love again allows us to do better and be better with the second chance.

Happiness comes from within. Sometimes our happiness lies deep beneath hurt and pain. Usually we see it as it is emerging but the potential for happiness is always there. At times, our happiness is the rainbow that comes only after the rain has fallen; however, most will agree that the beauty of a rainbow is undeniable. Most of us would prefer a sunny day and cloudless sky to a messy rain and residual rainbow.

Similar to the weather, some of the obstacles that we will face are unpredictable and beyond our control. How we deal with and grow from disappointment, grief and pain will chart the course of our respective life journeys.

Had it not been for the unfortunate losses in my young adult life, I would not be who I am today. The theme of my undergraduate graduation was Carpe Diem, which means seize the day in Latin. At the time of my college graduation carpe diem meant nothing to me. I recall ignorantly thinking, why would they pick something like that? Less than nine months after Aunt Sandy had come to my graduation, she was gone forever. Carpe diem means everything to me now. If my being, my very existence, inspires others to seize the day while living their dreams, then I will have accomplished my life's goal of making a difference in the lives of others.

About the Author
Natasha R.W. Eldridge

Natasha R.W. Eldridge, M.A. is a parenting and education expert, speaker and visionary entrepreneur. She is the founder and president of Kid Care Concierge, a company focused on managing and restoring balance to the lives of busy families.

For the past twenty years she has been leveraging her expertise in educational psychology and business to families, nonprofit agencies, schools and corporations. She assisted thousands of students who were deemed "at risk" to successfully complete high school and plan for a productive life after secondary school. President Bill Clinton personally commended her in 1999 for her work with urban youth. In 2005, her success was documented when she was interviewed for and quoted in *Whatever It Takes: Transforming American Schools—The Project Grad Story*.

Ms. Eldridge has appeared on the World News with

Diane Sawyer and was featured on HelloBeautiful.com. Natasha R.W. Eldridge has contributed as a family and parenting expert to publications such as My365 Lifestyle Magazine, Cafemom.com, and allParenting.com.

Natasha holds a bachelor's degree in psychology, a master's degree in educational psychology and is a Goldman Sachs *10,000 Small Businesses* alumnus.

She lives in New Jersey with her husband and their two daughters. Ms. Eldridge enjoys reading, traveling and volunteering as a life and business coach to young adults in her free time.

To book Natasha R.W. Eldridge, contact press@nreldridge.com, or locate her on Twitter: @natashaeldridge or LinkedIn: @natashaeldridge1.

How Champagne Tastes Help Your Love Life
Rachel Russo, MS, MFT

Once upon a time, a sassy young woman said, "You were my cup of tea, but I drink champagne now." This was, of course, considerably after Madame de Pompadour famously said, "Champagne is the only wine that leaves a woman beautiful after drinking it." As for me? Well, I'm no Madame, but I tell it like it is: Every woman deserves to sip champagne in a fancy dress—even if she has a beer budget, and the dress is from H&M!

Truth be told, most women settle for a $7 glass of house wine at the local dive, or worse, the can of Keystone chilling in the nearest gas station's convenience store refrigerator. Granted, some of these women just haven't been exposed to fine wine. They are young, inexperienced, and have no idea what they are missing. Others have sipped champagne with the best of the VIP crowd, but usually feel it's impolite to request something so special. For instance, when they are on a date, they don't want to order champagne and let the guy think they are high-maintenance. *Like that is a bad thing!* Sadly, there are a lot of women who don't believe they are worthy of such pleasures in life. Somewhere between being picked last for dodgeball and going to the prom without a date, they started walking around with a whole lot of weight on their shoulders. They got the idea that they don't deserve Moet.

This "weight" that many women carry is in the form of

41

self-limiting beliefs about love and life. One thing is for sure, such negative belief systems are destroying the self-esteem of modern-day women like the plague!

Perhaps the biggest factor contributing to women's low self-esteem is unhealthy relationships. First come unhealthy relationships with family, and then come unhealthy romantic relationships. We've all seen the latter. Whether we've watched a battered woman curled up on the floor of a bad *Lifetime* movie or in our own household; whether we've been out to dinner with that couple that makes everyone uncomfortable or whether we've been that couple—we have been intimately acquainted with a relationship that is less than functional. While most of us know that everyone doesn't have the same idea of what makes an ideal, healthy relationship, there are some things everyone can agree are just wrong.

But how does a relationship become so black and white that it is clearly wrong? How do the dynamics become so messed up that there aren't even any grey areas? How do you go from telling all your friends you're in love to not being able to tell a single soul about the kind of relationship you are really in? How do women who were once strong and confident begin to lack the self-respect that should have prompted them to kick their men's asses to the curb years ago?

While no two women have the same story of how they ended up in unhealthy relationships, there are often parallels—overlaps in their chapters, so to speak. As a Dating and Relationship Coach who was clinically trained as a Marriage and Family Therapist, I find that this makes sense. With my profound understanding of this systemic school of therapy, I see individuals' problems in a larger context. For example, if a client comes to me for advice on how to deal with a cheating husband, I don't automatically conclude her husband is a sociopath or sex addict who can't "keep it in his pants." I don't assume he is a dysfunctional human being who fails at life; I look at how the "system" has failed him. I consider how his family of origin may have contributed to his infidelity. Did his father cheat on his mother? Does he have friends who cheat on their wives? Is he part of a culture in which infidelity is the norm?

The reasons for unhealthy relationships can be seen through many lenses. In many ways, unhealthy relationships are products of the times, cultural problems, and even regional problems. Sometimes they are even a combination of the three. Like millennial men texting someone else's girlfriend while working a hedge fund on Wall Street, anyone?

Where do the stories of romantic relationships start to go wrong for young women? Well, it often starts with the quintessential teenage experience I mentioned earlier—the prom. You know, the one event that causes teenage girls to have panic attacks over decisions like wearing their hair up or down and whether to lie in a tanning bed or get a spray tan. This may be one of the first times a girl is objectified, not to mention pressured into sex. Grown women still talk to me about their experiences at prom!

Then, of course, there's college. If a girl goes away to live at a dorm without having been objectified in high school, she is pretty much guaranteed that it will happen here. For many college females, school is all a drunken blur of one hookup after the next. But it isn't just the casual sex that is unhealthy. It is the no-strings-attached fantasy that deludes the girl into thinking 1 a.m. booty call is what she actually wants. *Because she can be the "cool" girlfriend, eventually. And who needs titles these days anyway?*

Fast forward a few more years to sexual harassment in the workplace by male coworkers who have one too many at happy hour. Some women even have to deal with the CEO who gets a rise out of having affairs with interns in the copy room.

***

Somewhere after those first few years of starting a career in a big city, a bad breakup, and a dating marathon that can rival my own ninety-two-dates-in-one-year stint as Ms. NY of 3six5dates.com, a single woman steps into my office. She nervously fills out my application, both excited and scared of what will come of her first matchmaking or relationship coaching consultation. Part of my application may be familiar to her, as there are similarities between it and the registration form on a typical online dating site. I ask her to tell me about herself, what she does for work and for fun, and most importantly, what she's looking for in a relationship.

"Should I put my real age?" she asks.

I already know this woman. She's the one who is used to shaving off a few years just so she can come up in the searches of the youth-obsessed men she thinks she would like to date. But she tells me not to worry, since she fesses up after the first date. I tell her I don't blame her. I am all-too familiar with how ageist even the oldest of my male clients can be. I mean, it's all good until you are about twenty-nine, when men start thinking about your ticking clock. Even the silver foxes who don't want to have children insist on dating a minimum of ten years younger! The men all say they look young for their age and need someone who can keep up with them. *Sure. Cue to the part where I just smile and nod.*

As we sit down for some real talk, I learn about all the negative chatter that hijacks her mind on a regular basis, telling her of her limitations. The conversation reminds me of all the women who have sat here before her, beating themselves up and questioning the types of relationships they are worthy of.

They all say similar things:

"If only I was 10 pounds thinner…"

"I shouldn't have texted him first…"

"I wish I made him wait longer to sleep with me…"

"Every guy I've ever dated has cheated on me. It must be me…"

As her story unfolds, I learn of the pressure she feels from friends, family, and even strangers. They constantly ask:

"Are you dating?"

No, she's not. At least, not dating successfully, or she wouldn't be meeting with me! *Duh.* A lot of the time, a woman's family doesn't know she's sought out a professional matchmaker and relationship expert for help to find or keep love. She doesn't tell them, because she's embarrassed. She feels like they wouldn't understand. They'd say she's too picky, or that the right one comes along when you stop looking. They don't understand why she's single, so I become her dirty little secret.

And sometimes, our first meeting requires a box of tissues, since it serves as a reminder of all the failures of her love life. Surely she's had enough of those reminders! There are her ex's engagement photos popping up on her Facebook news feed, the closed conversations on the Coffee Meets Bagel dating app, the unread messages on Match.com, the lonely birthdays, the lack of a male counterpart to kiss on New Year's Eve, and the chocolates only from Mom on Valentine's Day. *Sigh.*

When I ask this woman about her relationship history and dating patterns, I hear about the "ghosts of boyfriends past" and the unhealthy "relationships" that were aborted after date #3. Of course, after ten years in the dating industry, I have heard it all!

"I usually date guys who are a lot younger…" Not surprised that's not working out for ya!

"I tend to go for the bad boys…"

"My last boyfriend drank a lot…"

"I had three Tinder dates yesterday, and two stood me up."

"I really had no idea he was bi. Do you think he's gay?..."

This woman's story isn't any better than the others I've heard. I'll have to tell my client that at the end of the day, her current interest is just another immature, narcissistic alcoholic who is such a player that he might leave a girl for another woman—or man!

Oh, I don't mean to sound so negative. I'll tell her that too! We have an understanding!

I know she gets that I'm just poking fun at the dating jungle, because, yes, there are a lot of men out there who are wild animals. "They will suck you into unhealthy relationships and then spit you out, but only if you let them," I say.

She nods, because she knows. She's a woman, and I will hear her roar! She is strong—even when she is weak!

***

Listen up, lady, because you ARE that woman. Whether you are single or coupled, whether you are feeling as strong or weak as ever, you are one with her! Just because you have been in an unhealthy relationship does not mean you have to be in an unhealthy relationship in the present or in the future. You have the power to change your world.

Indeed, there have been countless women before you who have survived and thrived after the most horrible relationships. I've not only heard their stories but have also become a part of their stories, as I coached them through some of their darkest times. I've taught them how to mend their broken hearts and get over their exes. Italian-American Style, to be exact. But I digress; that's a whole other book!

The women who have worked with me throughout the years have inspired me. They have done things that seemed impossible and blown me away with their courage. They have warmed my heart with stories of how they learned to love again. Ultimately, it is these special females who have allowed me to share this universal truth:

Sometimes, we ladies need to love an unhealthy man or two. We need to go through some unpleasant things before we can fully enjoy life's pleasures with a real, emotionally available man who will love us like we've never been loved before. With him or without him, we can be beautiful on the inside and on the outside—and even more so with the help of the finest champagne!

About the Author
Rachel Russo, MS, MFT

Rachel Russo is a Dating Coach, Matchmaker, Image Consultant, Author, and Speaker. With a master's degree in Marriage & Family Therapy from Iona College, a BA in Psychology from Rutgers University, and a certification as an Intentional Relationship Coach, Rachel has worked in the dating industry for ten years and has published two books as well as countless blogs. Since publishing her latest book, *How To Get Over Your Ex: A Step By Step Guide to Mend A Broken Heart Italian American Style*, Rachel has been acting as a Breakup Coach, helping diverse singles live happily in an ex-free zone. Rachel has also matched up lots of singles and was voted one of NYC's top twelve best matchmakers in 2014 by DatingAdvice.com. Rachel once went on ninety-two dates and blogged about them as Ms. NY of 3six5dates.com. More about Rachel at www.RachelRusso.com.

The Ultimate Deception and Betrayal
Regina Butler-Streets

This story is by a woman and her family who survived and overcame her husband's betrayal. As I tell my story, I can validate that Jesus Christ is real and prayer is the foundation of my life; these facts have been tested and proven for me.

Women usually desire an agape love—a genuine, unconditional love—from men. In the quest to find a good man, women seek certain essential characteristics. Typically, they search for a man who is committed, God-fearing, fatherly, loyal to his family, protective, providing, and encouraging to his wife and children.

I can honestly say I have never pursued a man; that activity was not common in my household. I was taught that God sends men to women. My primary focus in life was serving Christ and my community and pursuing my education. Nevertheless, if God should send a man, I would be honored to be a friend, and perhaps date when permissible.

As a child, I spent countless hours with my mother, a host of my aunts, and the matriarchs in my family. They provided me with the wisdom of God and knowledge of the characteristics of being a lady of God. An elderly woman from Sardis Baptist Church located in South Georgia was also a positive role model and mentor to me. She and I met after church services over a cup of warm tea to discuss the Bible and Jesus Christ. We discussed the pursuit of independence as a lady and what the most suitable man of God should look like. If I did date, it would have to be a man of God, someone who loved the Lord, and was capable of loving me. I learned that prayer was the answer to all life's anticipated challenges.

Immediately after high school, I remained focused on my education and career path. I credit the quality of my goals and accomplishments to my spiritual mother and mentor. My goals were to complete college, continue to work diligently in the church, and pursue my corporate career. I earned my Bachelor's degree in Business Management from Georgia State University. As a Human Resources Manager for fifteen years, I received several promotions. I remained involved in the community, attending several youth events. I was a member of Toastmaster and the Society for Human Resources, and I was very engaged in my family life.

On one fateful day, while working, I met a gentleman who appeared to have all of the God-like qualities that I desired. He said all the right words and spoke of raising God-fearing children. He was gentle, kind, attentive to my every need, and supportive of my career and future plans. Jacob entertained all of my heart's desires. He attended certain events just to see me smile. We attended the Fox Theater, the art museum, went on walks in the park, and participated in church services. He even expressed an interest in becoming a minister.

Prior to dating, we had to get approvals from our immediate family members. I drove Jacob to South Georgia to meet my Grandfather Jones for approval. He approved, but warned me to keep my eyes open. To my dismay, my father and my father's pastor in South Georgia did not approve of the relationship. Regardless of their thoughts and opinions, I decided to proceed with the relationship.

It was important to us that we were clear about our expectations for each other in our relationship. I informed him that I did not support drug use, consumption of alcohol, open relationships, physical or emotional abuse, smoking, or interference from extended family members. We also discussed having children and agreed that we would raise them together without input from our family members. I drafted a dating contract on the same day that this conversation took place. We both signed the contract in 1993.

The two years we spent together were great! We were active members in our church; we traveled and enjoyed several culinary experiences from New York to South Georgia. The final step before marriage was to meet his parents and family members in Pennsylvania. We planned a trip to meet his parents for approval of our intended marriage. When I first met the family, they reminded me of the Huxtable family in *The Cosby Show*. His entire family welcomed me and gave their blessings for our marriage.

We returned home to Georgia and began to plan our wedding. We set the date for November 11, 1995 and planned to have an intimate wedding with special friends and family members only. I was so happy and excited about spending the rest of my life with Jacob and I wanted everything to be perfect.

While planning for our wedding, I began to research places to live that would be good to raise our future children. Jacob would often say, *I will leave that to you, because you are good at that; I am not*. I felt honored that Jacob would allow me to oversee the choice of our future residence and educational system of our unborn children.

Though I planned for children, we both agreed not to have any until I graduated college. Jacob already had a son that I loved dearly and he appeared to be a wonderful father. Since we didn't want to care for children full time at this stage of our lives, we planned visitation for him and for Jacob to play an active role in his life. However, I expected that Jacob's son would continue to live with his mother.

Jacob and I got married in Conyers, Georgia, like we

planned. Some months later we spent our honeymoon in the Bahamas with Jacob's friend Mike and his soon-to-be wife. Prior to traveling to the Bahamas, I became ill. My physician informed me that I was pregnant.

During our time in the Bahamas, I noticed that Jacob was a risk-taker; he would often not follow the rules of the resort. The travel guide strongly suggested that we stay on the resort and not venture out alone. However, there were a couple of times Jacob and Mike ventured off the resort against the advice of the tour guide. One evening, Jacob and Mike decided to leave the resort to attend a party. Even though I was strongly against Jacob's decision, I allowed him to go anyway. There was another time when they chartered a boat to venture to another part of the island. This particular area of the island had a nude beach.

When Jacob first told me about his plans to go to the nude beach, I wondered to myself, *Why would a man of God want to travel to such a place?* Mike was not a Christian and Jacob was not being a good example of how a Christian should act. I began to pray for our return home and hoped Jacob would then prove to be the man that I had dated prior to marriage. I was afraid that he would no longer have respect for rules or authority.

At that point, our honeymoon was over for me, and I was ready to travel back to Atlanta, Georgia, immediately. I became deeply concerned for our marriage and for Jacob. I wondered if I could trust the man that I had chosen to be my husband. It was my hope that once we returned to Atlanta, I would have the opportunity to address these concerns.

I waited two weeks after we returned home to have a discussion with Jacob. I wasn't sure how to confront him about my feelings, since we were newly married. I decided to ask him how he felt about being married. He did not respond and appeared as if he did not want to have a discussion about our marriage. I told him that I wanted to talk about our honeymoon and how unhappy I was about some of the things he did. I reminded him about our faith in God and the commitment we made to each other, and that I did not approve of him going to a nude beach, especially while we were honeymooning. Jacob claimed that he was having a good time and that I should be more flexible in these matters. However, I stood firm in my standards.

April of 1995, Jacob's parents came to visit us in our first home. I was excited and happy to have them visit with us. When they arrived, we picked them up from Hartsfield-Jackson Atlanta International Airport. Something strange happened once we got to the airport. Jacob decided to get a rental car and drive his mother back to our apartment alone. Jacob's father drove back with me. During the drive, his father asked me several questions regarding our marriage. I shared with him that Jacob and I sought different ways to learn more about each other and that with Christ all issues could be resolved. I also told him about what Jacob did during our honeymoon, but he told me that men will always have their share of fun. I found his response to be inappropriate for a man of God.

Once we got home, my in-laws got comfortable in front of our fireplace and sipped wine. I told Jacob I wanted to speak with him in private and reminded him that I did not want alcohol in our home. Jacob felt that I was being negative and that there was nothing wrong with drinking a little wine. I was firm in my beliefs. I told him to tell his parents that I did not condone the consumption of alcohol and ask them to stop drinking it in my home.

When we returned to the living room, my in-laws asked us if Jacob's son could live with us, because his mother was not doing a good job of taking care of him. This question baffled me, since Jacob and I had never discussed potentially raising his son. I could not believe his parents had the audacity to ask us to take care of his son during our first year of marriage. It became clear to me that my husband had discussions with his parents that I was not privy to. I was livid and immediately became silent, because I had nothing to say. Jacob and I needed to talk about this without his parents present. I no longer trusted my husband. I was married to a stranger.

During breakfast the next day, my in-laws asked Jacob if he was allowed to travel outside Georgia by himself. I looked at them in bewilderment. Jacob told them that he would not be traveling during our first year of marriage. I found my in-laws to be strange and meddlesome, and believed that they encouraged him not to honor his marital vows. When the Bible speaks of like minds, it is true; you cannot operate in life with people who do not have the mind of Christ. I learned this biblical passage the hard way.

I was relieved when his parents finally left our home. Afterward, Jacob and I had a huge debate regarding marriage, and I was not happy with some of the things he said. I immediately realized that he was not the man for me and that I wanted to end this marriage as soon as possible. Once I came to the realization that my marriage was over, I did not have anyone I could express my feelings to, because I was ashamed. Instead of getting a divorce, I stayed in the marriage for fear of being a failure and because of my belief in God. I remained silent and hoped that maybe things would get better.

Our marriage did not get better, so I channeled my focus into my career and my child. I prayed that God would not grant me any more children with Jacob, as he had proven to be an unfit father and husband. It was a shameful request of God, but a realistic one. Prior to marrying Jacob, I had a good life filled with joy, peace and happiness. I had to remind myself that Christ provided the peace I needed.

Right after I gave birth to our son, Jacob lost his job at FedEx because he did not follow the rules. He had been with the company for twelve years, and, unknown to me prior to our marriage, he'd had incidents of substandard work performance with FedEx in the past. This behavior was similar to the behavior he had exhibited in the Bahamas. It seemed as if Jacob's erratic behavior was increasing day-by-day.

I was very unhappy. We no longer talked and we were rarely intimate with one another. Even with all that was going wrong with my marriage, a part of me wanted to save it. I worked in the Human Resources department, so I knew what counseling services were available to me as an employee. Even though I was embarrassed, I decided that Jacob and I should speak with a marriage counselor. Deep down inside, I felt that Jacob had a mental imbalance and I thought marital counseling would be able to diagnose his issue. However, our marriage was already at the point of no return, and Jacob was nonchalant about attending marital counseling.

During our first year of marriage, my stepson came to live with us. I was a new mother and needed Jacob's assistance with raising two children. But as I expected, Jacob was not available as a husband or a father. I encouraged him to spend time with his son, but he preferred to hang out with his friends.

My life with Jacob was miserable and his parents made it even more so. When we first started dating, we agreed that we would not allow our families to interfere with our marriage, but I quickly realized that the man who signed our pre-dating contract was someone other than the man I married. Jacob's mother was not only meddlesome, but also did not respect the vows of marriage. I believe that she encouraged her son's infidelity by having other women contact him at our home. They pretended to be cousins.

Jacob was out of control as he continued to disrespect me as his wife and the mother of his child.

One day, I came across a Mother's Day card that he purchased for one of his old girlfriends. He did not even buy a card for me that year. I confronted him about his relationship with his ex-girlfriend and he told me that they were still friends.

Every day was a new adventure with Jacob. I did not see an end in sight and I did not know what to do. One day, I came home from work to a house filled with smoke, because Jacob left food cooking on the stove. Jacob was too busy spending time with his girlfriend to care that our home was almost destroyed. Jacob found a new job after FedEx terminated him, but was eventually fired from there too. Jacob still pretended like he was going to work every day. I only found out he had lost his job when I contacted the company one day to talk to Jacob about our son and was told that he no longer worked there.

When I became pregnant with our second child, I began to fear Jacob. One day out of the blue he asked me if his son's mother could stay with us while she was visiting Atlanta. When I disagreed, he fiercely charged at me, causing me to fall on the floor. Once I regained my balance, I charged back.

I was at my wit's end and reluctantly called my friend Mary to tell her what was going on in my marriage. She encouraged me to call the police, but I did not listen. I was living and sleeping with Dr. Jekyll and Mr. Hyde, and the mere thought of him touching me made me feel ill.

Eventually I stopped sleeping with Jacob and he tried to use the Bible to convince me to sleep with him. We were living a lie. As much as I wanted to save this marriage, I knew that it was over. I needed to focus my attention on leaving him and buying a home for our children.

It took me some time, but I eventually saved up enough

money to purchase a home in Gwinnett County. I told Jacob that I would not be renewing the lease on our apartment and that he needed to find someplace else to live. Instead, Jacob told his parents that we had found a home and invited them to go and see the new home I was buying. I told him, "You should be happy that I know Jesus." His parents arrived in Georgia and thought the home was nice, but too large. This was the first time in my life that I did not have any respect for my elders. Taken by surprise at their level of immaturity, I did not show them disrespect, but only prayed for them and their son consistently.

I asked God for strength every day to end my marriage, but I could not. After many years of marriage and several marital counseling sessions, I tried to maintain our marriage for the benefit of our children. I wanted them to have their father in their lives.

We were a good-looking couple on the outside, but internally I was extremely unhappy and did not know how much more I could bear. Jacob's drug and alcohol abuse issues, which he had also hidden before our marriage, gave me concerns for my family's well-being. I prayed and asked God to allow me to be there to watch my children grow into healthy adults who possessed integrity, honesty, and morals.

When my children recognized their father's shortcomings, I would often direct them to pray for Daddy. I tried to hide the fact that he did not financially take care of his family and was mentally abusive to our children.

Once, my father heard Jacob threaten to hit our eight-year-old daughter. My father was very upset and was about to contact the police to have him arrested. I intervened and stopped him from alerting the authorities, because I did not want to send my children's father to jail. It became apparent to my family and friends that even though I was educated and professional, the life that I tried to present to them was a big lie.

Prior to my recent divorce proceedings Jacob and his family made no attempts to be an integral part of my children's life. They did not call or send cards or gifts for my children on their birthdays. I gave Jacob and his mother in particular ample opportunity to bond with my children, but they opted not to. I did not want my children to be a pawn in their game of manipulation and deception.

As a mother, it was ultimately my responsibility to protect my children from harm, so I made sure that they never visited his parents' residence alone after I found out that Jacob's mother gave alcohol to my seven-year-old child. I did not approve of their alcohol consumption and long nights of playing cards, and I did not trust them around my children. She displayed behavior that was unbecoming of an elderly Christian woman. Even though she attended church every Sunday, her spirit was demonic. The dangerous behaviors that Jacob exhibited stemmed from his mother. I prayed for her and left her behavior up to God. Eventually, I began to bring a family member with me when we visited my in-laws, for their living standards and drug and alcohol abuse made me fearful of them as well. I devoted my time to prayer and supplication often.

In 2009, the doctors at Gwinnett County Medical Center diagnosed Jacob with terminal cancer. I contacted his family in Pennsylvania about the diagnosis, but no one bothered to come to Atlanta to see him or offer support. It was clear to me at that moment that Jacob's family was unstable.

I was heavily involved in the church community, and there were several churches that prayed for his speedy recovery and healing. I stayed by his side and managed the home and children. I was accustomed to doing this anyway. I would ask God why He added additional burdens on me, and He reminded me that He always does things for my good.

Our finances were compromised as a result of Jacob's hefty medical bills and the Butler and Jones families helped us get through this difficult time.

Even though Jacob caused a lot of pain in my life, I didn't want him to die. I began researching doctors and hospitals that specialized in the type of cancer Jacob suffered from. Emory Cancer Center was highly recommended and I transferred him there. While Jacob was under their care, his cancer went into remission.

In 2011, Jacob announced that he was unhappy with our marriage and requested a separation. I granted his request. I coordinated a conference with our supporting pastor of several years, my parents, aunt and uncles, and my best friend from Virginia. Once again I drafted a contract. This contract outlined why he was requesting a separation and his financial obligations to his children. I booked his flight and told his mother to pick him up from the Philadelphia airport.

I am thankful to God for never allowing me to become mentally unstable or even suicidal during my marriage. I thank God for His strength, because I know it was not my own personal strength that allowed me to survive. Although the children and I had many months of tears, we found peace in our home. As soon as Jacob left, the joy of laughter returned and we were able to freely communicate with one another as a family. Most importantly, we continued to serve Christ in the midst of our storm.

I returned to college to pursue becoming a civil rights lawyer. Because of this choice, my son and daughter grew more eager than ever to reach new academic heights. As a family, we became more involved in our community by working with the youth and supporting single mothers.

Even though Jacob and I are divorced, he continues to be manipulative and deceitful. He moved from Savannah, Georgia, to Atlanta to seek joint custody of the children. He is currently living with the same girlfriend he bought the Mother's Day card for in 1999.

I am thrilled about what God has in store for me and the children. I know that He is not through with me yet. I have been blessed to work on numerous new youth and literacy projects that are geared towards helping children. It is my sincere hope that one day my children will be able to share their stories about survival and how God covered them during the storm and enabled them to persevere. Storms are a means of God's testimony. Ronald, Brandon, and Victoria Streets are my testimony of God's power.

It has been a privilege for me to be able to share my story and I hope that others will truly benefit from God's love and protection just as my family did.

I dedicate this chapter to my children: Ronald, Brandon, and Victoria Streets.

About the Author
Regina Butler-Streets

Regina Butler-Streets is an authentic Georgia Peach and Christ follower; she has lived in Atlanta, Georgia, since her early youth.

She is an accomplished Human Resources Executive with credentials in employee and labor relations, HR compliance, employee handbook development, personnel policies and procedures, compliance training and development (sexual harassment, wage and hour, Americans with Disabilities Act, and HIPPA). Her professional Human Resources Management experience are in both the Corporate Fortune 500 sector and TSA Homeland Security. Regina has a Bachelor of Arts degree in Human Services from Georgia State University and is an aspiring civil rights attorney at John Marshall Law School.

Regina's focus on community collaboration has led her to a

number of community leadership roles in youth advocacy, school-to-prison pipeline and education reform initiatives. She has been a guest speaker and panelist for the following events in Washington, D.C.: "We Can Do Better," Senator Durbing's hearing on Education Reform and School-to-Prison Pipeline, and the panel on ESEA Reauthorization, Civil Rights, School Discipline, and Students with Disabilities with Senator Murphy. She also served as a speaker during the Educational Reform conference in Portland, Oregon.

Regina partnered with Elaine Roberts, PhD, Associate Professor of Language and Literacy and Jill Drake, EdD, Professor of Mathematics Education at the University of West Georgia to develop "Rethinking Literacy and Math," an innovative and inspiring community-based program.

For the last five years, Regina has been an active participant in an outreach ministry to provide biblical instruction, words of inspiration, and songs to the seniors of Delmar Gardens Senior Living Center. She also participates in New Life community outreach programs.

I thank God for these blessings.
Regina Butler-Streets

Getting Up to Zero
Catherine Mossman

At the age of twelve, I felt unwanted in my family. I decided I needed to run away from home and find another place to live. At first I moved in with other families of kids I barely knew. I quickly learned what kind of people take in runaways without contacting other appropriate adults. This kind includes brothers, uncles, fathers, and friends of the family who would sneak into the bedroom where I was sleeping, put a giant hand over my mouth, and drag me out of bed and somewhere out of the way to have sex with me. One of those places was often a car. I still can't look at an El Camino without feeling sick. Whenever I "told," I was asked to leave. I learned not to "tell" until I had another place to go first. Otherwise, I would be forced to crash in someone's abandoned fort in the woods or with another undesirable. Despite these challenges away from home, I believed the ones I faced at home and school were worse.

By sixth grade, I was over school. I was over the daily harassment of Team Captains arguing over which team was going to "get stuck" with me. I was over the daily denied sleep-overs because of my chronic bed-wetting. I was over my mom getting other moms to force their kids to come to my birthday parties. Being in the bottom three shortest kids in the entire West Palm Beach Florida public elementary school, I was bullied until the trouble escalated to such epic proportions that a "small town meeting" of sorts was called. Teachers, guidance counselors, other school officials, about one hundred children (some of whom bullied me on a regular basis), and I all gathered in the school conference room. The worst bully, Donna, said all the right things, then kicked me in the shin on the way out the door with a smile. I was done with school after that and stopped going.

Mom and Dad had their own issues to preoccupy them. They thought, conveniently, that it would build character if I had to figure mine out by myself. Maybe it did.

When I was fifteen, my parents were divorced, and Dad was frequenting a local strip club… at least I think he was. I stayed with my dad, and my two younger siblings went with Mom and her new husband to be in Boca Raton, Florida. One stripper lived with my dad and me for a very short time, and a beautiful hooker was frequently on the scene.

Dad made my living with him very stressful on me. I didn't see it that way at the time. I was the eldest, and taking care of my dad was going to happen, without question!

Dad's behavior grew less and less appropriate as time went on. One day, while watching TV on the floor, head on hand like a typical kid, Dad threw a small magazine by my head… the *Penthouse edition/Forum Magazine*. It was filled with sexual fantasies and real sexual stories from readers. One story was "dog-eared" for me to read. I did as I was told and was panic-stricken to read a story about father and daughter sex! Over time, we went from Dad telling me to ask grocery store clerks to have sex with him, to waking up in my bedroom with Dad watching me, to sitting on his lap before bed for nightly kisses only to feel an erection underneath me, to reading a sexual story about a father and daughter. *I better get the hell out of this house,* was my overwhelming thought.

Blonde Barbie Hooker chick was happy to offer me a way out if I joined her profession, and at fifteen, not knowing any other way, I agreed. She had me perform a trial run on her male "friend." I "passed" and expected to be picked up and taken away the next day after I gathered my belongings.

However, while I said good-bye to my only confidant, Donna, the clerk chick at the local 7-Eleven, she offered me a way out. She just so happened to be leaving the next day for Cape Gerardeau, Missouri, where her family lived. Donna told me that she was going to take me with her. That day, we went to my house and threw my clothes in a garbage bag and she took me to her trailer.

That same night, Donna had a male guest who brought cocaine in hopes of a greater score with her. I went to sleep in the bed she made me outside the trailer in the screened-in "carport". It was raining. I was sound asleep when I woke to hear him leaving the trailer…unsatisfied. In a fast, heavy, mind-spinning whirlwind, he attacked me with all his pent-up frustration.

He took me and lashed his furious blows, which quickly ripped through my body. Without a word, he lifted himself off me and left in the dark, never to be seen again. A hole in the roofing material was letting water in.

As I lay stunned and ripped open, not even conscious of how he got my clothes off, water dripped on my head like a Chinese Water Torture scene in a B-grade war movie. I knew to remain silent. It was many years later before I felt safe enough to allow the screams that still lived within my cells to be heard.

The next day we left for Missouri. Donna's and my first stop was a place in Florida to stay with her brother to rest. I liked him and was thankful for how kindly he treated me. Wanting to express my gratitude the only way I knew how and believing sex was all I had to offer, I did my best to seduce him. But Donna interrupted before anything happened. No woman had ever intervened before, and it felt good to have someone care about me like that.

We left the next morning. When we arrived at her parent's huge duplex, her parents, her brother, his girlfriend and their new baby lived on one side, and Donna and I lived on the other side. Part of the agreement she made with her parents was that we all had to attend the local First Church of God with Donna's grandparents every Sunday. I was saved at the church revival and baptized at the river the next Sunday.

Within the first week, I was being sexual on a regular basis with both her brother and her uncle. Since they were authority figures who controlled my access to food and shelter, I didn't object or tell anyone about what they were doing.

However, my sexual escapades were discovered, and I was soon arrested for being a runaway at the church annual turkey shoot. The authorities brought me to the local juvenile detention center. They flew me back to Florida within days, my little white Bible in hand.

This time I went to live with my mother, stepfather, and two siblings in Boca Raton, Florida. Mom enrolled me in high school. Can you say, "total misfit"? I only really went to one class, the one George was in. I liked him. He gave me his leather jacket one day when I was cold and he never tried to have sex with me. He was always kind.

I wasn't in school very long before George's birthday arrived. George, two other boys, and I skipped school and went to George's house, because there was no "pot" to buy at school and there was alcohol at his home. Once school ended, we all had to return home to keep up the façade that we had gone to school. The boys decided to take me home first and then gather kids up for a party that night. George was on one motorcycle with a friend behind him, and the other boy drove me. We did that on purpose so we could talk privately about a gift for George.

Within thirty minutes I was watching George's bike slide sideways, with his body skidding down the asphalt one way and the rider bouncing off the road in another direction. I got his helmet off and his face was blue. I tried mouth to mouth…nothing.

I ran to the closest house and walked right inside to find a woman in a towel. "Call an ambulance now," I said. George was dead on arrival.

The next day I went to school and met up with my driver. As the misfit, everyone found it easy to blame me for George's death. Girls looked at me and screamed, "He died because of you."

The following day was Friday and Dad's weekend to have me. On the way to his place, he said that my mom had told him she didn't want me anymore. I was too wild.

When we arrived at Dad's place, I jumped out of the car and raced inside the house to call mom. She was unapologetic. I would be staying with Dad. *Lovely*.

Soon Dad and I were headed back up to Maine, like we did every early spring. I was thrilled, because I loved Maine. I felt safe in the woods and I loved the lake, where we had chickens and ducks.

When it was time to go back to Florida, I decided I wasn't going. A girl-friend, Tina, promised I could live with her and her boyfriend until I got on my feet. The night before Dad left for Florida, I once again filled up a black trash bag with clothes.

Soon Tina's boyfriend, Rick, picked me up…without Tina! He said that he had arranged another place for me to stay. That night I would stay at the Wagon Wheel Motel in Saco. I barely slept. I felt betrayed by Tina and worried about Rick's plans for me.

The next morning he picked me up, again without Tina, and drove to the Biddeford Court House to meet a man named Paul. Paul came to the truck window, looked at me, and shook his head in agreement. I got out with my bag of clothes and got into Paul's car. He drove us to his basement apartment on Pike street in Biddeford. As soon as we were inside, he ripped off my clothes and raped me. Paul was a drug dealer. This was his apartment and his rules. I was in a lot of trouble.

I wasn't there long before I met two girls who had their own apartment in the same building. We became friendly. Once, one of the girls hitchhiked to New Hampshire to visit one of her boyfriends, and the driver of a fancy pimped-out truck asked if I wanted to ride along on the three-day trip. I said yes. Sex in exchange for food and a pair of jeans. He gave me some cash, and I bought the girl's kind, poor family a steak dinner.

The girl's family let me stay with them when I was too afraid to go back to Paul's place. They were so poor and barely had enough food to feed themselves. Many meals were fried potatoes with catsup and hot tea. We slept at least two to a bed.

After the truck ride and steak dinner, the two girls gave me an offer. They told me that there were two possible pimps who could keep me in a safe, nice apartment and make sure I'd have enough food. They would protect me. I'd just have to have sex and give the money to them, and they'd take care of everything else for me!

Sounded good. I was taken to meet the two men; one black and one white, named Salt and Pepper. The black man was handsome, funny, big and strong. The white man wore glasses and had a lazy eye. He had a very thin line mustache, outdated and creepy.

There was no particular reason why I picked the white man, Salt. Peter was his given name. I later realized this was another "God" job. I soon witnessed Pepper's girls disappearing for days at a time only to be seen again bruised with a cast on an arm. Pepper had his girls hang out at the local Greyhound bus station on St. John Street and lure troubled girls to go with them. They had houses in Massachusetts, where they would imprison the girls, rape them, force them to have sex with dogs, and sell the movies on the black market.

My guy was new to the pimp world and only had a few girls. He tried his hand at abuse with me by hog tying me for an hour, but the most effective technique he used was brainwashing… creating invisible handcuffs of fear. He told me terrifying stories, which I believed, to keep me from escaping. Truthfully, even now at fifty, I'm afraid that he will find and kill me as he promised.

Prostitution is a subculture. It has its own rules. It has its own punishments. It is above the law.

Once I opened the door and two black men stood there. I let them in, even though MY pimp wasn't in, and that broke a rule. Within two minutes I was on the couch being raped by two men who were looking for a reason to break my bones. I surrendered and lay like a sack of potatoes. I didn't utter a single sound until they left me there bleeding and in shock. Fearful that Salt would do to me what Pepper did to his girls that broke the rules, I was terrified.

Another time I was sold to a hunting party of five staying at the local Holiday Inn. I was to meet other girls there, but no one else showed. I think one man bowed out, but the others went for it. One man bit me so hard, he broke my skin over and over. If I cried out, he bit harder. One man was nice enough to make him stop. I don't remember how much money Peter made that night.

I can't believe that over the years I never got pregnant or contracted a disease. I stopped menstruating.

My self-help journey began at the halfway house that took me in when I escaped from my pimp at sixteen years old. It was an alcohol rehabilitation facility, so I told the truth about my life story, but added drugs and drinking to my list of addictions so they could justify letting me stay there. I went to group and individual therapy sessions, in addition to twelve-step programs. While I was married, at seventeen years old,

I went to Alcohol Anonymous and to a fundamental church daily for a very long time. Twice a week, I went to individual and group therapy for women diagnosed with panic disorders for a year.

At the AA meetings, I met two men, Steve and a young handsome cowboy named Don. Don or Steve would bring me to the meetings most days. I liked Don because he never made a move. He was very kind to me and I wanted to show him I appreciated him…because I truly did.

The time came that Don and I were alone at his place after an AA meeting, and I made my move. Don used a condom and I was rarely having a menstruation cycle, so I wasn't worried about pregnancy at all. The condom broke. I was sick within days and I KNEW I was pregnant. I don't know how, but I KNEW. A woman from AA took me to her doctor and the doctor confirmed it.

I told Don. Don sat me on his lap and told me he loved me and would've asked me to marry him anyway. He asked me to marry him and get an abortion. I told him I would marry him but I would not get an abortion. I knew that an abortion would certainly be the one thing that would send me off the deep end, because I would never recover from killing my baby. With or without him, I would have my baby.

Don and I were married on December 26, 1981, in his parents' farmhouse surrounded by my family and his. His family was not happy, but that they put on a good face. His grandmother pulled me aside pre-wedding and told me to back away from her grandson.

During our marriage, Don did not have compassion for my pregnancy pains. When I would get sick in front of him, he would tell me that the pregnancy was my choice so he didn't want to hear any complaints. Sex stopped as soon I got visibly pregnant. He was twenty-one years old; fat women and infants were not his idea of a good time. He was gone…a lot.

Two years later, I asked for another baby so little Don (our son) could have a sibling. Reluctantly, my husband agreed.

Don was also an active Peeping Tom. He was turned on by the thought of what he couldn't easily have and turned off what was readily available. He didn't want to have sex with me, even though within weeks of having our children I would be back to one hundred pounds. After eight years of marriage, Don left me for another woman. We were divorced in April and he was married in July.

It wasn't until my divorce at the age of twenty-six that my self-help games really began. I went to a Church of Religious Science in Huntington Beach, California. It was there that I first got turned on to new thought and metaphysics. After that, I went to EST/ Landmark Education/ The Forum. I started attending lectures by Ram Dass, Marrianne Williamson, Wayne Dyer, Caroline Myss, and Wayne Muller to name a few. I also went to new thought churches like Unity and attended women's retreats. My self-help included being vegan for nine years, considering food as medicine. I did "rebirthing" and energy work, hypnotherapy, EMDR, Tapping, transcendental meditation and I attended The Hoffman Process, the Gay Hendrix breath work weekend workshop, the Sonia Choquette weekend workshop, and vast and various methods of therapy. Anything that claimed to heal trauma…I was all over it like white on rice. I went to the The Meadows and did the trauma work of Pia Mellody. I went to the Dalai Lama's World Peacemaking Conference and listened to Sharon Salzburg and the Levines.

I read anything written by Scott Peck, Louise Hay, Gerald Jampolsky, Sam Keen, Pema Chodren, or Calvin & Hobbs. I belonged to women's groups, incest survivor groups, and codependent anonymous group. I taught adult basic education classes at my Unity church. I did Lyengar yoga. I used exercise to help manage my panic symptoms. I did a lot of volunteer work for good karma. I was nothing shy of tenacious when it came to my healing journey. I heard them when they said I could have an amazing, love-filled and abundant life if I could change my mind. Game on!

Work was always an attempt to merge helping others with helping myself, from hospice type CNA/HHA in private homes, to work with a holistic lawyer who practiced family law and mediation, to national sales where I made a six-figure income on commission alone. I even went to school for a time to try to become a Unity minister.

While working in sales, I bought my dream house. Over time I walked away from that job to return to my heart's desire to help and give back…and here I am.

Today I am a speaker and writer. I also consider myself a photo artist, taking unique pictures of the Maine woods. I spend my time educating others about child molestation, bullying, sex-trafficking and overcoming trauma. Recently, I met with Governor Paul LePage.

How did I get from my rough beginning to here? As I write these words, I am fifty years old. I own a lovely little house five feet from the lake in Southern Maine. I volunteer at the local juvenile detention center's girls unit and speak at halfway houses. I have two wonderful adult children and four beautiful, happy, and healthy grandchildren. Charlie and I have been together four years now and plan to marry soon. As I write and sit on the dock here on Sebago Lake, there is a beautiful moon out. I look at the moonshine on the water and feel the warm, humid summer breeze on my skin.

I am in two worlds at once, the one from my past and the one I am in now. I am filled with enormous gratitude for the health and well-being that I am blessed with. The decades of self-help I tenaciously sought out, and like to think mastered, have paid off. Now, it is my highest joy to share the tools that I have acquired to move beyond the trauma and abuse, and to not be defined by or debilitated by the past, but to thrive. I've created a sanctuary within my own being, a home within myself.

For years I suffered with PTSD because of all of the abuse. I strove to be free from panic, nightmares, anxiety, and depression. Now I wake up happy almost every morning! I no longer wish I could die a hell and karma-free death. I have a great life, and I'm happy! I'm healthy. I have fun, and I have great friends. I have purpose and meaning, and I am free from panic.

I am thrilled to share everything I've learned with others in hopes of lessening the severity and duration of the suffering in others.

I quickly learned that there is no "arrival" after abuse and trauma… it's a journey. It's a life-long journey, and there are two ways to travel it…in kind, honest, compassionate joy, or in fear and panic. I have found out how I can travel in joy… and I am so grateful!

About the Author
Catherine Mossman

P ippi Longstocking, carrying a stuffed, over-loved Pooh Bear, dressed up like a FABulous drag queen, with no shoes and extra lip gloss, dances around the bonfire before she falls asleep on a dew-soaked twin mattress that Charlie dragged out to the end of the dock. He did this so she could sleep outside, watching the shooting stars, and meet the sunrise unobstructed by the confines of walls.

***

Catherine survived decades of abuse and subsequent debilitating PTSD, seemingly relentless anxiety attacks, and low-grade depression that made walking through life feel like Atreyu walking with his horse, Atrax through "the swamp of sadness" in the movie *The Never-ending Story*. Like the fictional story… most do not survive the journey.

For more information about Catherine, visit: www. catherineamossman.com

I Can
Stephanie Snowe

Thanksgiving has always been my favorite holiday. I love the turkey and the pie, the time off school and work, and the visits with family. But even more than all of that, Thanksgiving always meant a beginning to me, the start of the holiday season.

I enjoyed looking at all the glossy ads that came in the newspaper, making my wish list, and dreaming about what was to come.

In November 1997, I had even more dreams than usual. Not only was I looking forward to the holiday season and everything that came along with it, but also I was pregnant with twins. I eagerly anticipated seeing their faces for the first time the following May. Although I was young, I had medical problems, which had plagued me for years. I never thought I would be able to have children, and I was excited about being a mother.

I have to admit I was a bit nervous about having two babies at the same time, and although he never talked to me about it, my husband seemed to share my fears. He spent more and more time at work, rarely talked to me when he was home, and started sleeping on the couch. He said it was so he wouldn't disturb me, but my doubts began to overshadow his words.

On Thanksgiving morning I woke up early and listened to my husband snoring in the living room for a few moments. Something was wrong. I had been denying it to myself for weeks, but I decided I could no longer ignore my feelings. I went into the living room and sat on the floor in front of him.

When he opened his eyes I asked, "What's going on? Really?" I was not prepared for his answer.

"I don't want to be married to you anymore."

We had been married only a little over a year after dating for three and a half years. We bought a house together and planned to have a child. True, it was a shock for both of us that our plan hadn't exactly worked out the way we intended, but I believed twins were the miracle we'd always prayed for.

He's just scared, I told myself. *He'll snap out of this soon.* The weeks slipped by and the truth came spilling out in ugly chunks. It wasn't just that he didn't want to be married anymore. It was that he didn't love me. That he'd never loved me. That no one loved me, not even my own parents. No one cared about me. I was worthless. I was fat. I was not going to be a good mother. No one would ever want me.

Every day that he spoke to me, another barrage of verbal assaults came out. He spit out the words, as though they were so disgusting he had to get them out of his mouth as fast as possible. Every time he talked to me, it was to say something horrible or degrading, anything that could make me feel like less of a human being.

One day after he was particularly harsh and hurtful, I snapped back at him, "Someday, you'll regret saying these things to me. One day you'll look back and wish you hadn't done this."

His response dripped with sarcasm, "Oh well." I will never forget the cruel look on his face as he said those words.

My pregnancy was difficult, and I was extraordinarily ill. I lost thirty pounds during the first few months of pregnancy, partially because I was so heartsick it was difficult to eat, and partly because when I did eat, my body would rebel. Morning sickness never went away, becoming all-day sickness. I had several episodes of bleeding which required me to be hospitalized and monitored. Toward the end of my pregnancy, I developed toxemia and rapidly gained a great deal of weight.

Often, I paced up and down the narrow hall of my small house, crying out to God. I just wanted someone to acknowledge what was happening to me. Instead of the anticipation and excitement of pregnancy, I felt nothing but anguish. I decided that once my children were born, I would just kill myself. There was no reason for me to live. *If I couldn't even be a decent wife, how could I ever be a decent mother?*

I gave birth alone in March, via an emergency cesarean section, to a boy and a girl. My daughter looked like a tiny, perfect doll. My son looked frighteningly fragile, far too small and weak to be in this world. I didn't know if he would live or die, and at first the doctors weren't sure either.

This time in my life was gray. It was a maze of hospitals and doctors, of not enough sleep and far too much worry. I felt stupid, helpless, and hopeless. I believed that everything my husband said to me was true. I wasn't good enough. I couldn't even carry a baby the right way. I'd done something wrong that made this happen. I didn't deserve anything good. I couldn't kill myself though. I couldn't bring myself to do it.

I knew in my heart that despite what he loudly protested, my husband would not be a part of my children's lives. I knew that it would be my responsibility to care for these small people, and I could not cause them pain. I knew that, even though I didn't want it to happen, my husband was going to divorce me. The laws in the state in which we lived prevented pregnant women from getting divorced, so my husband filed for one shortly after the children were born, while they were still in the hospital fighting for their lives. His life without the three of us was continuing, no matter what.

Right after my children were finally declared well enough to leave the hospital, my dad drove his green van to my house, loaded up as many things as he could—including me and my children—and drove us back to North Carolina. I was getting a new start, whether I wanted it or not.

The day after I moved out, my husband's girlfriend moved into the house with him. He denied her very existence and insisted I was crazy, but she was there, sleeping in my bed, eating off my dishes, and watching the television I bought. She left her husband of many years and her two kids, and stepped right into my life like I never even mattered.

"Oh well," indeed.

For about a year, I went through the motions. I found a daycare and a job. I made small payments on the staggering medical bills I owed, found a doctor for my children, and steadfastly ignored the divorce paperwork I wasn't quite able to deal with.

I applied for WIC benefits so I could afford to feed my son the extremely expensive formula his sensitive stomach required. The shame I felt when a cashier couldn't interpret my coupon and shouted over the loudspeaker that she needed a manager to help with some food stamps has never left me. I politely pointed out that WIC wasn't food stamps, and she sneered at me and said, "Same difference!"

It wasn't supposed to be this way. I was trying so hard, but I was still so far behind. My soon-to-be ex-husband paid a pittance in child support, not even half of what was required to pay a monthly daycare bill for twins. Eventually, he paid nothing at all.

I was so busy keeping my head above water, I completely forgot about committing suicide. I didn't have time.

I made friends at my job, and met men who wanted to take me out on dates. They didn't care that I had children. They thought I was smart and funny and beautiful and told me so.

I wasn't ready for any of that, and frankly they should have cared that I had children, because my children were always going to be more important than anyone I dated. I did go on dates sometimes, but mostly they were just a distraction in my life.

Right then, I couldn't imagine ever getting married again or ever trusting anyone enough to try. I just wanted to raise my children, who were becoming funny and bright and were by far the best parts of my life. It was becoming easier to forget how hard everything had been and how unimportant I was.

The marriage ended in September of 1999. I could no longer avoid it. I went to the courtroom alone. The judge asked my now ex-husband what the birth dates of our children were and their middle names, and he didn't know either. I felt like I would vomit. After a year and a half of working so hard, of doing everything I could, of not having any support, of knowing he had cheated on me and lied about it, and of knowing he couldn't even be bothered enough with his own children to know what day of the year they were born, I was done. It was over. I was free and I was tired.

I started looking for a better job, one that would offer insurance. I didn't want to have to rely on anyone else for insurance for my children. I found a new job the very month after the divorce was finalized. I received my own office with a nameplate on my desk. I made more money—not a lot, but it helped.

I decided I would achieve my goals first, get my life figured out, and then, eventually, I would see if marriage was something I ever wanted to do again. Although it seemed very scary to me, I did not believe that marriage had to be bad or painful. I believed that, just maybe, there was someone out there for which marriage and commitment would not be a struggle. I saw examples of happy marriages around me. They weren't perfect, but other couples were able to work things out and stay together, so I started to believe that maybe I could be half of a couple who could too.

My grand plan started out as dreams in my day planner. I would write down the dollar amounts I wanted to make in a year, the jobs I wanted to have, and the qualities of the person I wanted to be. It seemed so big and scary looking at them on paper, but plans often start as dreams and evolve into so much more. I wrote down what I wanted, even if it seemed unattainable, and then read it every day. Eventually, I was ready to start taking action.

I wanted to buy a house on my own, with no help from anyone. I wanted a place that would be in my name only and that I could decorate any way I wanted. I knew it wouldn't be a dream mansion, but something would be better than nothing. I saved my pennies and found a little white townhouse with two bedrooms that seemed like it would be just right. I was nervous when I applied for the loan, even a little sick. What if I couldn't do this? I'd never applied for such a large loan by myself. I'd never even dared to think I could. The loan was approved, and I felt dizzy when I signed the paperwork. Dizzy, but proud.

My kitchen was purple and so was the bathroom, just because that's what I wanted.

I was not happy with my job, but I knew I could not get a better job without a college degree, so I went to a local community college and took all the testing required for entrance. I had to sit down with an admissions counselor and as soon as he said, "How are you?" I started to sob. Even though I knew he must have thought I was crazy, I couldn't stop crying.

What am I doing? I can't do this! I was so scared. I had a full-time job and two kids and I had no idea how I was going to add college to the chaos that was our life. I also didn't know if I could pass math.

As he handed me a tissue, the admissions counselor told me I could. He told me people did it all the time, and I could too. I'm still not sure why, but I believed him. This man didn't know anything about me except that I cried at seemingly inconsequential things, but I believed what he said to me.

After all, I told myself, I had two babies at the same time with no one in the delivery room to hold my hand, and a lot of people couldn't say that. I bought a house by myself too. I had a job and I was paying all my bills on my own. Maybe my ex-husband was wrong. Maybe I wasn't worthless after all. On a leap of faith, I enrolled in college that day.

My life fell into a very busy routine. I worked hard, studied, and spent time with my children, who were growing into funny, sweet, intelligent little people. When I looked into their faces, I knew I wanted better for them. I knew why I was working so hard. I wanted my daughter to know that if a man cheated on you or broke your heart, it didn't mean that it was the end of the world. That you picked yourself up and kept going. That love comes in many forms, and the purest and sweetest is the love between a mother and her children.

My heart was not broken, not completely. It was cracked, but the love of my son and my daughter were enough. They had always been enough, even though I hadn't always known it. The love I had for them filled me up.

Then, there was Jason.

I think I fell in love with him the very first night I met him, which is ridiculous. The whole thing was ridiculous. He was a boy, only twenty-two years old. I was twenty-three, but was already the mother of two children. Jason had decided fairly quickly that he was in love with me too. He spent time with my children and the rest of my family. He was supportive of my goals. He was funny, handsome, and smart, and he thought I was beautiful. He praised my cooking, although he'd worked as a chef for many years, laughed at my jokes, and valued my opinions. He was the complete opposite in every way of my ex-husband, and in December of 2002, when he got down on one knee and asked me if I would be his wife, I did not hesitate when I said yes.

We've been married now for over eleven years. He still compliments my cooking, loves my figure, and thinks I'm hilarious. He tells me what a good wife and mother I am. Our marriage has not been perfect, but I don't think marriage is supposed to be. He is my closest friend and confidant.

My babies are almost seventeen years old. They are brilliant, funny, resourceful, and sweet. They are very different from each other, yet they are the best of friends. They are honor students, well-liked by everyone they meet, and kind and loving. They still make me laugh every day, sometimes to the point that I cry, and my heart is so filled with love for the two of them that it sometimes feels like it will burst. I have made many mistakes in my life and done many things wrong, but my children prove to me every day that I have a purpose in this world. My life has meaning, and I am a good mom, no matter what my ex-husband thought.

Two days before my thirty-fifth birthday, my ex-husband passed away. He never knew my son and daughter. He never went to a dance recital or a choral concert. He never saw my son accept an ROTC award and never saw my daughter act in a school play. He was not there for any of their Tae Kwon Do matches; he never helped with their homework. He was not there when my daughter was baptized. He was not there when the two of them learned to ride their bikes. He missed every holiday and never even sent a birthday card.

My children were largely unfazed by his death. My daughter, displaying wisdom beyond her years, very succinctly said, "I'm sorry for his family," but did not include herself as part of it. They knew of his existence and had only minimal questions throughout the years. Jason is their dad. He is the only dad they've ever known.

Since my ex-husband's death, I've felt anger and sorrow,

an odd mix, but an important one for me to deal with. I have many questions that will never be answered. Sometimes a door closes and there is nothing you can do to re-open it. My anger at my ex-husband is sometimes unhealthy, but I don't hate him. I could never hate him, despite his cruelty, because every time I look at my son and daughter, I know that without him I would have never had the greatest blessings in my life. These days, I feel sorry for him. What joy he missed in his brief life, and for what? I'll never know now.

My children have always been my greatest supporters. Even now as teenagers, they are endlessly positive and supportive. My son and I recently took up running, and he constantly reminds me that I can do it. He says it doesn't matter if I'm slow, because I'm still up and going. I'm getting better. He mentions the muscles in my legs, and tells me how much I've accomplished so far. My daughter leaves me notes on my scale that remind me I am beautiful either way and not to bother with the number. If I'm having a particularly bad day at my work-from-home job, she passes me notes that say, "You can. Cry if you need to, but you can do this. You can get through this."

If I had allowed the anger and bitterness to win, my world would be a completely different place. I sometimes look back at my scribbled notes in my old day planner pages, and I just have to smile. I graduated college in 2006, with honors. My first book was published in 2009. I have a good job, and the dollar amount that I make annually far surpasses that dream number I wrote down so many years ago. I live in a lovely home that is filled with laughter, and I even have a sweet dog, who is my constant companion.

There are many people in this world who care for me and love my children. I give back to my community through volunteer work and try really hard to be a better person and a good example for my children. I've learned so much. I've grown. I am not perfect, nor is my life, but it is easy for me to see that I am blessed beyond measure. I could not imagine my life without Jason, nor do I want to, but it is a great comfort to me to know that should I ever wind up alone, for any reason, I can take care of myself and my children. There is peace in that knowledge.

Sometimes I imagine my heart as a cracked vase. It will never be perfect again. There are little leaks in it sometimes, and I'm sure it's not pretty. I still let doubts creep in occasionally, and there are times when I struggle with the little voice in my head that says, "Maybe you can't."

But oh, I can. I can.

With the love of my family as the glue to hold my broken pieces together, *yes, I can.*

About the Author
Stephanie Snowe

*S*tephanie Snowe is the author of *Meeting Mr. Wrong: The Romantic Misadventures of a Southern Belle,* and was a contributor to the book *Good Dogs Doing Good.* Her writing was also presented as part of the off-Broadway show *Are you there, God? It's me, Blogologues.* She makes her home in eastern North Carolina and also on the web at www.stephaniesnowe.com.

With God, Nothing Is Impossible
Katha Blackwell

Throughout my entire childhood, all I saw were women in my family being mistreated, abused, cheated on and divorced. So my hope for a healthy relationship was very dim. The only healthy marriage I knew of was that of a distant cousin I saw on special occasions and that of a couple on a popular television show. The relationship between Heathcliff Huxtable and Claire Huxtable on *The Cosby Show* is the relationship I dreamed of having, and watching those shows gave me a glimpse of a marriage I would one day have of my own.

The beginning of my childhood was rough. I saw some peace early on and I remember the good times, but I also remember the nightmares. The abuse between my parents I remember vaguely, but the abuse I experienced from my stepfather is what I will always remember. He was the nightmare. I didn't know what walking on eggshells was until he showed up at our door. Sadly, as a naïve child, I wanted a father figure in my life. I wanted the Brady Bunch. But he was far from that.

He met my mom at a jazz club, and that same evening he slept on our couch. Now being the people we are, we knew that having a stranger on our couch was out of order. It was strange to go from having no man in our lives to having one sleeping on our couch. My sister and I whispered to each other, wondering who this man was. What kind of man goes to the house of a single mother on the first night? Secondly, what kind of woman allows a strange man to come into her home with her daughters in the house? A woman who is foolish. We later found out that out of all the women he could have went with, he chose our mother, which began ten years of darkness.

This man was an absolute monster. He was abusive, a liar, and manipulative, and on top of all that, he was crazy. Throughout my childhood, I freely shared with other adults and family members stories of the abuse we experienced, but to my knowledge, nothing was ever done. This nightmare stayed with our family until I went to college. But instead of allowing it to get me off track in life, I used this situation to motivate me to keep moving forward.

When my sister left for college, I had just started high school. It broke my heart to see her leave. Not because my favorite sister in the world was leaving, but because I would have to endure the abuse by myself. However, I did not let that stop me. I decided to start a four-year countdown to college and allowed the abuse to motivate me to get out of that house.

At school I had friends who were also dealing with their share of drama. For some, the drama pushed them into a life of even more abuse, heartache, and disappointments. I started dating in high school and ended up being cheated on many times. I was motivated to leave any and all relationships that brought nothing but heartache.

Something in me would not allow me to believe that my future would be filled with abuse. After my mother finally divorced the man who had brought an overwhelming amount of abuse and division to our family, I told myself, "This will not be me." I started believing again that there had to be some good men in this world that didn't break hearts or beat women.

Life comes with a lot of ups and downs. Some we have control over and others we do not, but it is up to us to determine whether or not those down times will dictate our future. I was determined to not repeat history. Throughout the next four years of my life, I worked hard to get out of that house and I did. My motivation was peace. I wanted peace, and I knew that allowing this abuse to influence me to live a life of sin was not going to get me to a place of peace.

Everything that I experienced could have easily discouraged me. I could have started to believe that all men are cheaters and abusers, that all men will break your heart, and that marriage is a joke. But because of God, I was able to overcome those negative thoughts and press towards truth. The truth is that every man is not a cheater, liar, or abuser. Regardless of what I had seen, I still had hope in my heart. That hope is what kept me moving forward when everything around me was encouraging me to give up.

After enduring four more years of abuse, I finally left home. I went from Tennessee all the way to Michigan. Everyone kept asking me, "Why are you going so far?" My answer was always straightforward…Because I want to get away.

Once I got to Michigan State University, I majored in Political Science and Pre-law. My primary goal was to become a lawyer and prosecute abusive men. But while I was in college, I realized that the pain I had experienced followed me to college and I needed to heal.

I started reflecting on all the madness and foolishness the last fourteen years had brought. I mourned my childhood and questioned why I went through such a mess. I did not understand the point, and asked God for one continuously. Little did I know that what the devil meant for bad, God turned around for my good.

After connecting with an amazing campus ministry, finding some healthy friends, and staying single for a good minute, I began to heal. God provided me with peace and love from a family of friends I developed in college. They were friends who empowered me and became a light in my life.

I later took a course that allowed me to visit the homes of women who were either in an abusive relationship or had just gotten out of one. Visiting with them motivated me to focus on helping women heal from abusive relationships. I realized the experiences I went through were not in vain, but gave me the power to help someone else.

After college I worked at various domestic violence shelters and became a motivational speaker, author, and support group leader. I continue to be used by God to help others. The rough relationships I experienced were a stepping stone to my calling.

I married my college sweetheart and we have been married for over ten years. We have two beautiful children now. He has never abused me, cheated on me or broken my heart. My home is finally a home of peace and love—the way everyone's household should be.

Life is not always filled with good times, but when those bad times come, remember that they are only for a season. Continue to press forward and believe that God is able to restore every bit of joy that has been stolen from you. When moving on with your life, keep in mind the following:

#1 A healthy heart is a secure heart:

One of the craziest things I see women do after a bad relationship is immediately get into another relationship. This is insane! When your heart has been broken, it needs time to heal, just like every other part of your body. It does no good for anyone to jump into another relationship when someone in the relationship is still hurting. In order to heal, you need to take some time out and be alone. Do not be so quick to jump into the arms or bed of someone who can only make you forget about your pain for the moment. Write about what you feel, cry it out, talk with one of your close friends, pray about it and let it go. That is how you heal from bad relationships.

#2 Never allow the opinions of others to dictate your future:

There will be plenty of times in your life in which you will hear that all men are cheaters, abusers, etc. That way of thinking will get you nowhere. Most women who talk that way are still dealing with the pain they experienced, and instead of dreaming again, they would rather not dream at all. Do not allow their pain to dictate your future. However, you should learn from them.

#3 Follow your gut feelings:

There is something truly genuine about women's intuition. That feeling you get that tells you to go left instead of right even though for the last five years you have always gone left? Follow that! Follow that feeling that says something is not right, even though your man appears to be perfect. If on the first couple of dates, it seems like something is wrong, nine times out of ten there is something wrong. In every relationship you are in, you should be at peace. There shouldn't be any ill feelings if this man is truly the man for you. And if there are ill feelings, don't rush into this relationship. Even if it's the day of your wedding and you have hesitations, don't do it.

#4 Don't be afraid of being single:

Before I met my husband, I was single for two years and celibate for five. I had stopped being eager for a husband and stopped feeling like I needed someone in my life. All I needed was time to heal and reflect upon everything that happened throughout my life and get back to me. During that time I focused on my relationship with God. I needed to enjoy being alone so I could evaluate myself and learn about what true love really looks like. I went through the process of going to the movies by myself, going out to eat by myself, having movie nights by myself and gaining a sense of security within myself.

***

I encourage you to use these tips to help transform your life as a woman. Remember that a relationship or lack of one does not define you. Wait until you are ready and until the right man comes along. You are *worth* it.

About the Author

Katha Blackwell

Born and raised in Chattanooga, Tennessee, relationship expert Katha D. Blackwell knew at a young age that abuse was wrong. After years of seeing women in her family go through abusive relationships, Katha decided to make it her goal to help women.

After graduating from high school, Katha went to Michigan State University (MSU) and became one of the many field researchers for the Violence Against Women Initiative. As a field researcher, Katha visited the homes of abused women and collected data for a longitudinal study. In 2003, Katha graduated from MSU with a bachelor's degree. That following year Katha married her college sweetheart, Eric B. Blackwell, in 2004.

In fall 2004, Katha started graduate school at The University of Chicago (U of C) where she majored in Social Services Administration. Throughout her time at U of C, Katha maintained full-time employment at a local domestic violence shelter as a Residential Counselor, and fulfilled her field practicum requirements as a Family Therapist and an Adult Domestic Violence Counselor. Upon graduating with a Master's degree from U of C, Katha continued to work with victims of domestic violence, providing full-time individual and group counseling services.

The key reason Katha writes is because she wants to help better the lives of women. Katha has been a counselor, therapist, volunteer, and case manager, and in all those roles, Katha constantly had to sugarcoat the fact that bad relationships can be avoided. As a writer, Katha can be honest and give needed instruction to empower many women.

Her first book is titled, *Not Another Victim: A Woman's Guide to Avoiding a Bad Relationship*. Visit KathaBlackwell.com for more information and a monthly encouraging blog.

Katha currently resides in Georgia with her husband Eric, and their children, Elias and Eliana.

A Holistic Definition of Free
Lynn Fairweather, MSW

*N*ote: Although women can be abusive, men can be victims, and violence also occurs in LGBTQ relationships, the majority of systemic, injurious, and persistent domestic violence involves males perpetrators and female victims. Therefore, the following piece will use pronouns that reflect that statistical reality.

On most mornings, I wake up sure of where I am, of who I am, and of who is around me in the safe haven of my current life. But on occasion, when my eyes are still closed and my mind still saturated with dreams, I find myself back in time, at a two-story condo in a sunny southern state. Shadows are ever-present there despite the reigning rays, and I am trapped in the upstairs bedroom where he won't let me leave and he won't let me stay. His expression is twisted, his words like blades.

I awake as though coming up from underwater, gasping for air like my life is about to leave me. Dreams have a memory longer than that of the conscious brain, and even though it's been nearly twenty years since I've seen my abuser's face, he sometimes appears clearly to me in the darkness, even more sinister in my nightmares than he ever was in real life, and I wonder, "When will I ever be completely free of this experience?"

When someone asks me how I "got free" from the prison of domestic violence, I often wonder if that term means the same to them as it does to me. Do they want to know how I actually walked out the door, or how I gradually took my life back over the years that followed? You see, "becoming free" is a multi-step process, not an event. It has several key parts, each with its own complex course of development. Just like there are six forms of domestic violence, there are also six corresponding types of freedom from it.

The half dozen aspects of abuse I'm referring to are as follows: physical, sexual, verbal, psychological, economic, and spiritual. Each one of these has a corresponding "facet of freedom" that survivors can recognize on their journey toward safety and healing. There is no exact timeline for this progression because everyone moves through the course at their own pace. Sadly some may never make it to the finish line, as they constantly fall backward to retrace their own footsteps. Let's examine how each one of these areas can help us to determine a new and more complete definition of the word "free."

Physical Freedom

The first part of liberty from domestic violence comes when the victim is no longer in bodily danger from the abuser. Her former partner doesn't have the opportunity to attack her because they don't live in the same house/town/state/country anymore or the abuser is incarcerated, dead, or simply no longer shows any signs of intention to harm.

However, even after leaving an abusive relationship, many victims are still in grave danger. In fact, leaving ushers in the period of highest risk for an abused woman, as this is when her controller loses control, and may react with a violent attempt to regain it.

Some survivors never feel safe. Despite the passage of years and even decades, they are constantly looking over their shoulders or living underground to hide from individuals who have promised to hunt and kill them.

Fortunately for me, I doubt I'll ever see my abuser again. Although I've achieved physical freedom from his reach, I still operate on a reasonable plane of awareness and practice a low level of cyber tracking called "counter-stalking." The purpose of this online activity is to discover exactly where my abuser is in proximity to my location. Even after nearly twenty years, I always breathe a sigh of relief when the computer reveals that he still lives on the other side of the world.

Sexual Freedom

The second factor to consider in examining a more well-rounded explanation of "freedom" is sexual recovery and healing. Women who were sexually abused by an intimate partner may have a difficult time feeling comfortable and present in their own bodies, enjoying future sexual experiences, and learning to trust people again. They may have to battle traumatic memories or even physical scarring as a reminder of what has happened to them. Rape, forced prostitution, reproductive coercion, and other aspects of sexual abuse can color all the physically intimate experiences that follow, and survivors must work hard to reclaim their sexual sovereignty. Their benchmark of freedom comes when their memories no longer control their bodies, and the insecurities implanted by abuse disintegrate and float away under the loving warmth of a healthy relationship.

Verbal and Psychological Freedom

The third and fourth facets can be combined because they so often walk together under the umbrella of domestic violence. Liberation from verbal and psychological abuse can be surprisingly difficult to achieve because both require a cleansing or "deprogramming" process to counteract the brainwashing that the victim may have suffered for years. In the case of verbal abuse, the perpetrator systematically depletes the victim's self-esteem with constant insults and put-downs, so it will be that much harder for her to gather the strength to leave. The abuser may threaten the victim, lie to her, or poison her friendships, her employment, and her family connections. Even when they have ended the relationship and found safety, some survivors still hear the echoes of their abusers' voices, disparaging them at every turn even though the abusers are no longer in their lives. The true measure of verbal freedom comes when a survivor can say whatever she wants, speak to whomever she chooses, and express whatever opinions she desires without fear of retribution from anyone.

Psychological abuse, although just as detrimental, can be more covert than verbal abuse, because in order to psychologically terrorize his victim, an abuser never has to say a word. He can draw his finger across his throat or shape it into a gun. He can ball up his fist, or flash "the look"— the one every victim knows is the promise of a beating to come. An abuser can isolate the victim from her supporters, sabotage her professional and educational opportunities, or engage in "crazy-making" behaviors such as changing clocks or hidingkeys, all with the aim of making the victim question her own sanity and ability.

It takes time to recover from a mental beating, perhaps even longer than it does from a physical one. Sometimes the scars of the mind never fade at all. But when a survivor can sleep contentedly at night and get through her day without anxiety, she is well on her way to healing.

Economic Freedom

Economic abuse is a central factor in why many women stay in or return to dangerous relationships. When an abuser takes all of the victim's money, forbids her to earn any, or refuses to allow her access to bank accounts, he is solidifying her "chains" and diminishing the chances that she will leave the relationship. When he leaves her out of important money decisions, issues her a paltry allowance, and demands that she account for every penny spent, he is reducing her ability to be self-sufficient and independent. For some survivors, economic abuse continues far longer than the abusive situation itself. For example, an abuser who refuses to pay child support can financially punish his victim for years to come, while doing the same to their unfortunate offspring.

My abuser ran up my credit cards during our relationship, promising to pay them off once the bills came in. Of course, he did not, and I was left with a mountain of debt that haunted me for over a decade even though our relationship lasted no more than two years.

Spiritual Freedom

Finally, we look to the spiritual aspect of abuse and autonomy from it. Common tactics of spiritual abuse include forbidding a victim to practice her religion of choice, mocking her faith, destroying religious books or symbols, and alienating or threatening members of her spiritual community. Because many victims rely on their creeds and congregations to support them through the harrowing experience of abuse, it is all the more difficult if they cannot practice as they wish. It is also abusive for a perpetrator to claim that a religion permits or even condones intimate partner violence.

When a victim feels free to believe and worship (or not) as she pleases, and no longer has her spiritual side darkened by the shadows of fear, she can move forward and grow into a stronger human being. This will help her to recognize her self-worth and be less willing to compromise her own convictions in the next relationship she enters.

∗∗∗

Despite the occasional nocturnal reminders, and the few specific "triggers" that my abuser left me with, I still know from my lengthy career in domestic violence response and prevention that I was one of the lucky ones. Yes, I was physically attacked and psychologically tortured, but I still consider myself fortunate because I didn't have a lot of the challenges that other victims face. To begin with, my abuser and I weren't married, we had no children, and we owned no property together, all of which are powerful binders and barriers from escape. I had family that could (and did) help me financially. I knew the social service and criminal justice systems like the back of my hand because I worked as a domestic violence victim advocate. I was blessed because I am not mentally ill, disabled, addicted, or undocumented, all factors which could have prevented me from getting out. I was advantaged because I am white, cis-gendered, and college educated—all of which probably got me better treatment from cops, prosecutors, judges, and doctors down south in the early 90's. I was lucky because my abuser did not own a gun. If he did, I might not be here right now.

But most of all, the thing that truly allowed me to escape the hell I'd been living in was the fact that I wasn't in love with my abuser. In the beginning, I was impressed by his cosmopolitan charm, worldliness, and intelligence. But by the end I could see just how damaged he was, and I lost all affection for him and all attachment to our relationship. I can't imagine how much harder it would have been if I had still retained hope. If I truly wanted a future with this man, if we shared a family, a history, and a mutual passion that I couldn't live without - then it would have been monumentally more difficult for me to escape as I did and stay away forever.

When faced with a disclosure of domestic violence within a relationship, the first thing people want is to see the victim "get free." People often ask this question regarding women who remain attached to a dangerous partner: "Why doesn't she just leave?" They ask this as though doing so were as simple as it sounds. "If it were really that bad," they reason, "why would she still be with him/love him/voluntarily stay in that situation?" This inquiry is not only insensitive to the victim's position, but is also a bold assumption that 1) a victim is free to do as she pleases 2) leaving will solve the problem, and 3) the onus is on the victim to change what's happening.

Here's what most people don't understand about what they are suggesting:

Getting physically free is no guarantee of safety.

As mentioned previously, when the victim walks out, "the controller loses control" and may ramp up his negative behaviors in response. Some abusers kill their victim at the very moment she announces she is leaving the relationship. Others wait until she is packing her bags to react violently, or even stalk their target for months before attacking at her new apartment or the parking lot of her workplace. In one study, 55% of intimate partner femicide victims were estranged from their partner when killed (Campbell et al., 2003). Many abusive partners simply continue to track, follow, harass, and terrorize their victims to make them come back or to punish them for not coming back. For the victim, it can feel like a lose-lose situation from which there is truly no escape.

In order to take the great leap of faith that getting free requires, victims must have a safety net stretched out beneath them.

That security web is made from courage, self-confidence, and resilience, sewn together by the support of friends, family, neighbors, employers, and the social service and criminal justice systems. Unless the victim has made a plan and can clearly see that net below, she might want to hold off on jumping, because those who leave without adequate preparation can suffer financially, emotionally, academically, and socially, and they may end up having to return out of necessity.

Many victims have to practice "getting free."

The average domestic violence victim leaves seven times before they leave forever. This means that survivors need practice, they need to test the water and see how life will be on their own, and they need to know how their partner will react to their departure.

If you catch someone in the midst of this cycle, please don't lose hope or withdraw your assistance because they returned to the relationship temporarily. People remain in or return to violent situations for a variety of reasons, including fear, financial hardship, love, religious and cultural expectations, family pressure, poor health, or children. There is no one-size-fits-all prescription because each situation is individual and unique.

Victims must reach "escape velocity" before they can get free.

Escape velocity is the tipping point when the fear of staying outweighs the fear of leaving. For some women, that time comes when the abuser threatens or hurts their children. For others it is when they are badly injured for the first time or their partner is arrested. Regardless of the reason that brought a woman to that fateful place, escape velocity represents a point of no return, when a victim has finally decided to become a survivor.

In my abusive relationship, I wanted to leave long before I did; I just simply had no means to do so. Getting my own apartment would have required first month's rent, a security deposit, and furnishings. I was a full-time student with a part-time job that barely paid me enough to feed myself. The few friendships my abuser had not sabotaged by that time were flimsy at best, and no one I knew had the room to put me up anyway. I considered living in my car, but I knew that the touristy beach town around me had a dangerous underbelly. It wasn't safe for a nineteen-year-old woman to be on the shark-infested streets alone. So for almost two years, I stayed trapped with the devil I knew, because he was less frightening than the one I didn't.

Finally, after a particularly disturbing incident of violence, I laid down my pride and called my family to beg for money. Mercifully, they sent it, and I was able to get myself a rundown $400 a month apartment in the area of my school and work. But, like many victims, I soon realized that just because I was done with my abuser didn't mean he was done with me. He stalked, harassed, and threatened me for months, until eventually I left the state because I knew in my heart that if he could reach me, he would never leave me alone. Even afterward, living thousands of miles away, the process of "leaving" continued to draw out as I learned to calm my nerves, to trust people again, and to shake off all the sick feelings that accompanied that awful experience.

The following is excerpted from the epilogue of my 2012 book *Stop Signs: Recognizing, Avoiding, and Escaping Abusive Relationships* (Seal Press) with some minor edits for context. It continues a story from the beginning of the book that describes my post-beating conversation with a police officer, while I stood in a driveway covered with blood.

Just before the police car came around the corner, some well meaning allies presented me with a temptation many victims would jump at. The two male friends who intervened when my abuser attacked me had overpowered him and were holding him down in the yard as he thrashed and cursed. When I regained my senses after his barrage of violence, I walked over to where they were and they held him up in front of me, pinning his arms back in a "full nelson" wrestling move. "Go ahead," they offered. "Take your best shot."

I would be lying if I said I didn't want to punch him dead in the face. For once, I would get revenge for all the things he'd done to me and feel what it was like to be on the distributing end of violence instead of the receiving. But I quickly pushed that thought out of my head, because I knew I was better than that. I knew I was better than him. "No," I answered, looking him straight in the eyes. "You're going to jail tonight. I'm not." And he did.

In that moment, my whole abusive experience was framed for me, and out of that epiphany came my determination to rise above it. I learned that it wasn't about getting even or even about getting justice. It was about getting whole and deciding to save myself by walking directly through the fire and out the other side.

For survivors of domestic violence, being liberated is about more than just walking out the door. It's a holistic transformation in which they reclaim their own power from the people who stole it by strengthening and educating themselves, so that no one ever takes it away again. To me, that confident security represents the true and complete definition of *getting free*.

About the Author
Lynn Fairweather, MSW

Lynn Fairweather, MSW is an abuse survivor who has worked in the domestic violence response and prevention field since 1993. In her role as president of Presage Consulting and Training, Lynn is responsible for providing guidance and education to professionals across the country in both the public and private sector. She is an experienced and engaging public speaker, comfortable with audiences of all sizes and disciplines. Her well-received trainings are informative as well as interactive, with a focus on practical real-life skills for evaluating and managing domestic violence threats.

Lynn also creates customized domestic violence programs for organizations wishing to address the issue internally, and serves as a subject matter expert on a variety of projects. Before creating Presage in 2008, Lynn earned a bachelor's degree in Social Science and a master's degree in Social Work.

Her skills in domestic violence threat assessment were developed by providing direct service to thousands of victims through positions in social service, law enforcement/corrections, university, and shelter systems. Throughout her career, Lynn has served on several successful interpersonal violence task forces and response teams, and stands as a strong advocate for coordinated community action against abuse. She has facilitated many victim support groups and batterer's intervention programs, including those for incarcerated victims and for abusers within a parole and probation program.

Lynn is an active member of the Association of Threat Assessment Professionals and serves as board President for the Oregon Violence Against Women Political Action Committee. She holds multiple training certifications from institutions such as Homeland Security's Federal Law Enforcement Training Center and Gavin de Becker's Advanced Threat Assessment Academy. Locally, Lynn volunteers with non-profit domestic violence programs as a way of giving back to the advocacy field where she began her career. She also writes professionally on the subject of domestic violence and recently released her first book, entitled *Stop Signs: Recognizing, Avoiding, and Escaping Abusive Relationship*s (Seal Press 2012).

Unseen Scars
Amanda Pearson

Long after the physical pain is gone, the emotional pain remains among the torn memories of my life. The mistakes I made haunt me to this day. I scratch and tear at my strength and self-respect every time I am faced with the decisions that take my son from my arms.

These moments will remain in my life until my son is of age and no longer has to deal with two people who find it hard to dual-parent from two different states. I despise having to give in to a person who took a part of who I am away from me so many years ago. It is easy to disassociate myself from that man, until I have to make decisions affecting my son's emotional relationships with his parents.

I have strengthened who I am by formally educating myself, being honest with my family and close friends about what happened to me, and allowing people to love me—loving them back is the hard part. Or, I should say, letting them know I love them is the hard part.

I've grown to understand that being in love is different from simply loving someone. I love cats, dogs, music, and apple pie, but I am in love with my boyfriend. When you understand the difference between love and being in love, being afraid to be in relationships takes on a new meaning. It becomes the normal kind of fear of compatibility instead of fearing the person you "think" you are in love with is going to blacken your eye or take other women to bed. I say with absolute certainty that I have never been in love without fear until now.

A common misconception is that a person who allows herself to be controlled is weak or has low self-esteem. That is not the rule; that is the exception. I was looking for a strong and determined man when I met the person I will refer to as Armando. He had everything I thought I wanted and needed at that time in my life. We were both hard-working and going places in our careers. Armando was charming, witty, and extremely thoughtful. He pursued me for three months before I actually went out on a date with him.

The two years we dated wasn't what I thought love should be, but since we were taking care of business, I didn't mind. There were plenty of missed dates and disappointments along the way, but I kept accepting the excuses since he was "working." It wasn't hard to check on his stories, and for the most part, he wasn't lying about working anyway.

I wondered what I could do to make myself more important than his fraternity, his friends, or his baseball team. It was not the fact that he was doing all of these events that bothered me, but the favors and all of the extras that seemed to take precedence over me. If we had a date, then I felt as though he should honor our commitment or at least try to make it up the next day if he missed it. Admittedly, though, I liked a man who was a part of the community and who enjoyed helping his friends and co-workers. I thought it showed a caring part of an otherwise hard-to-reach character.

It wasn't until after I was three months pregnant that Armando changed into an extremely controlling person. He became very angry when I wouldn't do as he directed or when I disagreed with his opinions. My first taste of this came abruptly. We were moving my things from a house I shared with two other people, because I thought it was better to live in my own place once I had the baby. I was packing boxes and putting the lighter ones in my truck. It wasn't a problem until we got to the apartment. I unloaded what I could and started unpacking. Then it seemed as if a switch flipped in his head, and he began berating me for not getting the heavier boxes from his truck. "You are using your pregnancy to get attention," he said. "You are not one of those weak females who claim they can't do anything while they are pregnant, so don't start acting like one now."

I was shocked to hear those words pour from the mouth of the same man that encouraged me so many times before. Prior to this incident, he had NEVER spoken to me that way. I tried explaining that I had packed them too heavily and could not lift them. "I will not do that again so I can help more next time," I said.

That wasn't good enough for him; Armando kept on with the insults. I have never been one to allow anybody to talk to me in that way, and I wasn't about to start then. I asked him to leave and not worry about my things any longer; I would figure out how to move the stuff myself.

We both walked out of the apartment and I slammed the door in anger. Well, anybody who has dealt with a person with violent tendencies knows that action would be a trigger. I, on the other hand, didn't know and really didn't care. I didn't need him. I started driving back to my old house, and Armando tried to run me off the road. The man who told me he adored me and wanted to marry me was trying to physically hurt me!

There were a lot of things I should have done differently that day, but instead I tried to prove there was no way he was going to bully me, but I didn't. I drove faster, weaving in and out of traffic and not answering my cell phone. I thought he would exit the highway toward his house, but I was wrong. He was following me. My heart felt like it would beat out of my chest and I couldn't think clearly.

What was my next move? Should I call the cops? What had he done at this point for them to do anything? I didn't have any proof of his violent actions.

When I arrived, I jumped out of my truck and tried to run inside. He was faster and caught the door before I could get it closed. I forget now what words we exchanged, but the one thing I have not forgotten is the way he punched me in my face as though I were another man. He pushed me down, sat on my chest, and punched me. This wasn't the first time I had ever been tackled, since my older brother and I used to go at each other fiercely, but this time was different. This time I was being attacked by a man who was supposed to protect and love me.

I managed to pull myself free, run to the kitchen and grab a knife. He grabbed my wrist, squeezing so hard I couldn't hold on to the knife anymore. It fell to the floor. We pushed each other until he shoved me down to my knees and began punching me in my head. I didn't want to stand up, because I was afraid he would hit my stomach and hurt my baby. All I could do was lie on my back and kick his shins and knees, trying to get him to fall.

When he finally did, I ran to the garage where I kept my baseball bat. Swinging it like crazy so he couldn't get near me, I walked into the driveway. The neighbors were outside, and he left.

I never called the police. I am not sure why. Perhaps it was because we were both in the military and would have been labeled. A woman who "lets" a man hit her is viewed as weak, and others question her ability to lead if she can't keep her own life together. When a soldier becomes "labeled," she is denied responsibilities that could advance her career.

I didn't hear from him in weeks. I didn't have any marks on my face, just swelling and a migraine that lasted for days. I was raised in a rough environment with all boy cousins and an older brother, so being hit wasn't something new to me. Growing up, fights escalated from disagreements or when somebody took my toys and broke them. The only thing I could think I took from Armando was my permission for him to control me.

Armando had orders from the military that would soon force him to move away, so I knew his violence wasn't something I would have to deal with for long. Before he left, he asked to meet me for dinner to talk about our child. Up until that point, it hadn't occurred to me he would want to be a part of our child's life. At dinner he acted as though nothing had happened and as if we hadn't gone for weeks without speaking. I expected him to beg and apologize, like I have seen in movies and read in books after a man beats a woman. His behavior had me wondering what was going on inside his head.

He asked what we were going to do when our son was born. "How much leave do you think I should take? Do you think I should wait until he is born to come back to visit?" Realizing Armando's full potential for crazy, I went along with him.

I went along for another eight months after my son was born. I would fly to South Carolina from Texas every couple of months so Armando would realize we had something bigger than ourselves to prioritize, our son. We laughed and had great times.

Then it happened again. His insecurities about being a parent got the better of him and he started verbally attacking me. Never being the type of person to let people talk disrespectfully to me, I verbally combated this crazy man. What was I thinking? I wasn't. My need to show him I wasn't going to allow this behavior from him was greater than my intelligence. If I were thinking clearly, I would have let him vent and addressed the issue another day.

When the words "You are teaching our son to be a faggot" crossed his lips, I lost my cool. I was furious that this man could think that way about an eight-month-old child who sucked his thumb. How ignorant he was of human behavior, and the bigotry he possessed was disgusting. He began questioning my parenting and saying things that were relevant to my own doubts about being a mother.

I couldn't take it any longer and blurted out, "How would you know how to be a father when you are never around?" He chased me through the house, knocked me down, jumped on me, and began punching me in the face. I looked over at my son lying on the floor watching me, and I knew I had to do something.

Armando crawled off me, babbling, "You make me do these things. If you would just learn to keep your mouth shut, these things wouldn't happen!"

I didn't say anything. I had to get out of there before he hurt our child, my baby. I started packing my bags, still without saying anything. Armando stood in the doorway, arms crossed, and told me I wasn't leaving and I wasn't taking his son anywhere. I didn't stop.

He rushed over, snatched the clothes out of my hand and punched me. I saw blood dripping on the floor, checked my face, and realized it was coming from my mouth and nose. Some of it had been there a while because it was partially dry. I turned around, pushed Armando, and finally backed him against the wall with my forearm pushing against his throat. I begged him to stop.

Somehow we ended up in the bathroom, with me sitting on the floor crying and him yelling at me to stop crying. He turned out the lights and started punching me again. That was it. That was the point where it stopped.

I felt the cord from my curling iron on the floor. Pulling it down to make sure I had enough of it, I jumped up and wrapped it around his throat. I wanted him to stop the madness. I wanted him to be the man I first met. I wanted him to love me enough to protect me from things like this. He wasn't going to, so I considered doing something that would have made me worse of a monster than he was. But I couldn't become that monster; I couldn't kill him. When I finally let go, Armando dropped to the floor, choking and coughing. Without saying a word, he left the house.

I don't know why I didn't leave. I should have called the cops, but I didn't…again. There weren't any witnesses and I knew it would be his word against mine. I didn't want to be dragged in and out of court, talking to investigators, and potentially have my son taken away. Selfishly, I didn't want Armando's military career to be jeopardized either, because then he would have been financially useless to my son and me.

It was on me to make decisions that protected my son and me. It was easier to do what I had to do because I lived halfway across the country. I could pretend Armando didn't exist and worry less about him showing up at my job or home to harass me.

My son and I made it back home the next day, and I began the process of ensuring that monster never came near me again. I read articles about abused women who went on to succeed in life and have meaningful relationships. I wasn't a weak person and didn't have low self-esteem, which was how the articles categorized women who stay in abusive relationships. I wasn't uneducated, and I didn't accept what happened to me as something I deserved. Instead, I understood the man whom I thought I knew had mental deficiencies and didn't realize what he had when he had my heart.

Armando eventually became distracted with other women, didn't call as much, and moved on. He saw his son a few more times before he fell off the face of the earth for a couple of years. Eventually, he found a steady girlfriend who didn't understand why he didn't visit his son. The games were about to begin.

After years of no contact, Armando showed up on my doorstep, girlfriend in tow, and demanded to see his son. He threatened and insulted me and called the cops and my supervisor. My son wasn't even there at the time. This was only a show for Armando's girlfriend so she could believe he was the type of man she wanted/needed him to be.

During this time, he took me to court on various allegations of abandonment, neglect, and keeping him from his son. They were all lies that were eventually vetted in court. Yet he still found a way to hurt me: he abused me mentally and brought in reinforcements to validate him.

It is never easy being the person who always does the right thing. It takes a strong woman to say, "Enough is enough." It takes a stronger woman to put the past in the past and allow the future to exist.

Over the years, Armando continued to find ways to put me down and tell our son negative things about me. It hurt, but no matter how many times I wanted to call him and tell him how he was mentally abusing our son, I didn't. I maintained my composure for my son and reassured him that people say untrue things all the time and we have to learn the difference between ignorance and truth.

Armando couldn't keep up the facade very long, though, before many truths came to light. Eventually, he met a woman that fit into his world. As he dated her, he shared lies and half-truths about his life. After a couple of years, he deployed and decided to marry her before he left. When Armando later had an accident while overseas, his wife had to go through his files, papers, and personal information he locked up in a briefcase. She found his lies. She began an investigation, and everything came to light.

On a mission to repair the damage, she decided to see

if there was something inside Armando that was still good. He went to therapy and used medication to help the journey. Ten years later, through his wife's and my strength, endurance, and unwillingness to quit, my son has a relationship with his dad he can finally talk about with hopefulness and pride. I am no longer "the crazy baby-momma." I am no longer the horrible, delusional woman Armando portrayed me as.

I have learned many things throughout this time and, more recently, through the support of the man who has become my everything. One thing I learned is that you cannot make somebody else care about anything as intensely as you do. You will waste much time and cry many tears attempting to do so. Focus on how YOU want to do things, and do them in a manner YOU feel is right for the life you WANT. Never stop trying. Never allow people to dictate what you make of yourself. That is why it is called "self "... it is based on your own actions.

I read somewhere that "the fight begins after you survive." After you have crawled, walked, or ran away...the real struggle will begin.

Pray. The people that hurt you will continue to bring you down and attempt to hurt you in ways you would have never thought possible through harassment and deceit.

Pray. Smile when you really want to cry. Smile when you feel as though you can no longer go on.

And pray. Repeat the words "Please, God, help me" over and over again until you can no longer think about your problems anymore.

I have heard many people ask, "Why has God allowed this to happen to me?" That is something only God can answer. You have to be willing, and your mind and your heart have to be open. When you are ready to receive His answer, it will come.

About the Author
Amanda Pearson

Amanda Pearson is originally from Idaho. It was there she joined the military, which eventually brought her to Texas, where she currently lives. She has an eleven-year-old son whom she adores; he is her entire world.

For a while, Amanda pursued a degree she was not passionate about. She is three classes away from completing a Bachelor of Science degree in Computer Information Systems with Texas A&M, but she has always been fascinated with art, creating, and the design of almost everything. Since as far back as she can remember, her passion has been photography. She has a love of taking pictures and an appreciation of what others have captured artistically. She wants to be able to incorporate photography and design into her career.

Due to her passion for art, she chose to work toward a bachelor's degree in Graphic Design instead. She has been a student at The Arts Institute for sixteen months and has about eight more to go. She self-taught herself digital art, and is still learning all other areas of art. She is currently interning and doing some independent work to practice her digital skills. Another Arts Institute student demanded she draw every day if she wanted to get better, so Amanda tries to practice often. She is still working on being able to draw every day (Her fellow student would be disappointed in her for that).

She used to work full-time at a job that only fulfilled the need to make money. But she wants to be able to wake up in the morning excited about what she is about to do at work and not dread going into the office on Mondays. She loved every minute of the twelve years she spent in the military. Okay, maybe not EVERY minute, but she liked what she did and she was a good solider. Now, she is going to chase her goal of doing something she loves again, something she has wanted to do since she was a teenager.

Conclusion

One of the most important gifts that you have been given is the gift of life. Each morning when you wake up, you have another opportunity to live your best life. Your struggles and triumphs are testaments to the journey that you embarked upon the day you left your mother's womb. No, it has not been easy; yes, it has been challenging; but whether you know it or not, you haven't given up. Each day you wake up is an opportunity to do something different, to meet your challenges head on, and to witness the greatness of life. Life is a gift, so it is time to accept it as such and design a future that you deserve. You know you have what it takes. It might take some time, but with the determination and unwillingness to accept anything less than what you envision, you will overcome and conquer your fear. You will—I know it.

If at times you are not feeling your best, turn to one of the chapters in this book and find your source of encouragement; find your will to do more than you think you can. For if it were not for you, others would not be inspired, motivated, or encouraged to be the best people they could be.

We are all designed to share a piece of ourselves with others, and by being at our best, we get an opportunity to do just that. I want to thank the authors of *Tales of Women Survivors: How We Became Free* for sharing a piece of themselves to inspire and give strength to others.

Brighter Tomorrow

Susan Peabody

Life may take a downward spiral,
And overwhelm us for a while.
Pain may seem a way of life,
Endless moments filled with strife.
Gloom may settle in our soul,
Splitting that which once was whole.
And yet despite this painful rift,
There still exists a timeless gift,
The saving grace when all is gray,
The promise of a brand new day.